P9-DGT-911

Copic®
Coloring
Guide™

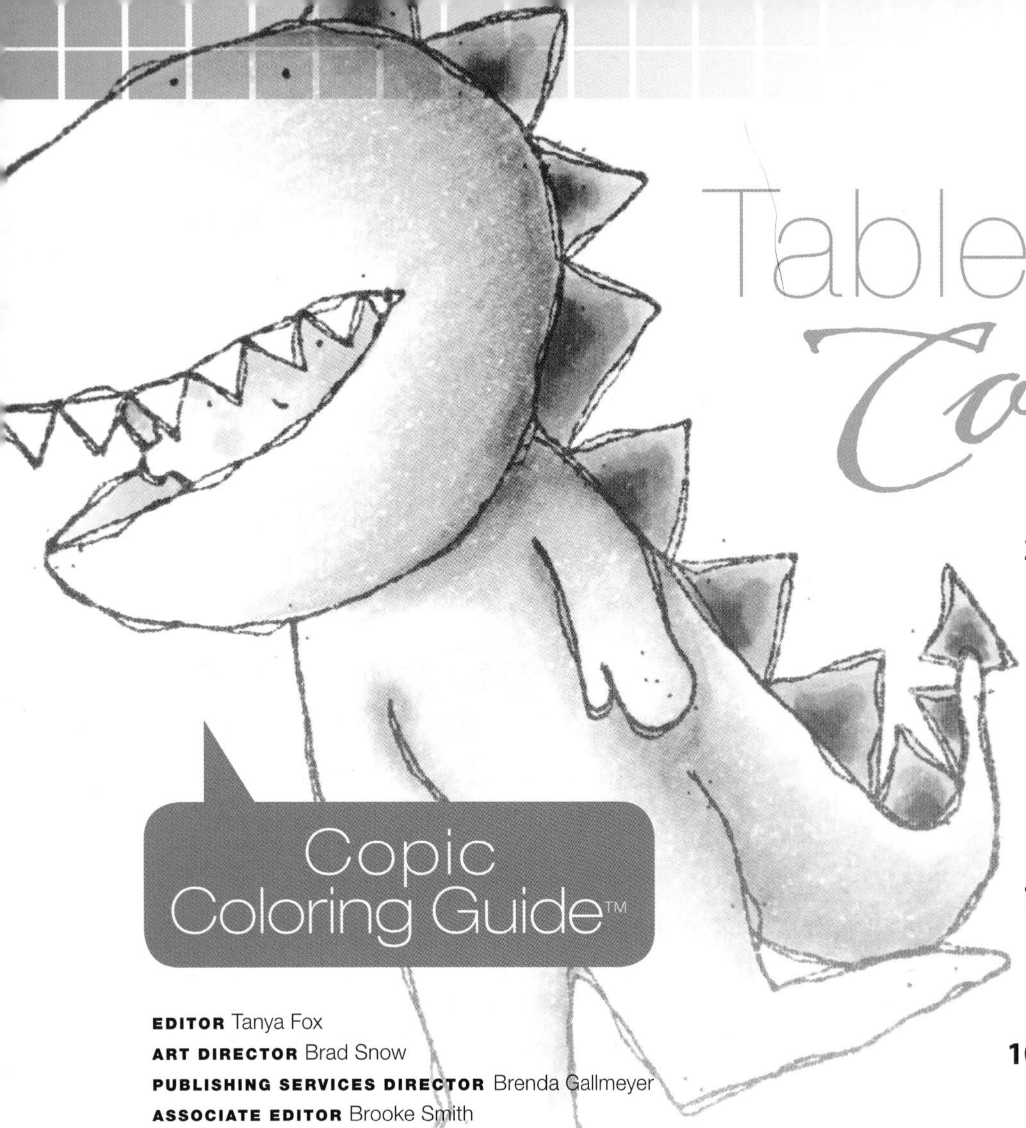

Table of Contents

EDITOR Tanya Fox
ART DIRECTOR Brad Snow
PUBLISHING SERVICES DIRECTOR Brenda Gallmeyer
ASSOCIATE EDITOR Brooke Smith
ASSISTANT ART DIRECTOR Nick Pierce
COPY SUPERVISOR Deborah Morgan
COPY EDITORS Mary O'Donnell, Samantha Schneider
TECHNICAL EDITOR Corene Painter
PHOTOGRAPHY SUPERVISOR Tammy Christian
PHOTO STYLISTS Tammy Liechty, Tammy Steiner
PHOTOGRAPHY Matthew Owen
PRODUCTION ARTIST SUPERVISOR Erin Augsburger
GRAPHIC ARTIST Nicole Gage
PRODUCTION ASSISTANTS Marj Morgan, Judy Neuenschwander

ISBN: 978-1-59635-376-3
Printed in the USA
2 3 4 5 6 7 8 9

Copic Coloring Guide is published by DRG, 306 East Parr Road, Berne, IN 46711. Printed in USA. Copyright © 2011 DRG. All rights reserved. This publication may not be reproduced in part or in whole without written permission from the publisher.

RETAIL STORES: If you would like to carry this pattern book or any other DRG publications, visit DRGwholesale.com.

Every effort has been made to ensure that the instructions in this publication are complete and accurate. We cannot, however, take responsibility for human error, typographical mistakes or variations in individual work. Please visit AnniesCustomerCare.com to check for pattern updates.

I found I could say things with color and shapes that I couldn't say any other way—things I had no words for.

~ Georgia O'Keeffe

Intro to Copic *Markers*

Why Copic?

It's simple, really:

- Top-quality product designed to be a lifelong art tool
- Variety of barrel styles to fit any budget/need
- Alcohol ink can be layered and blended without harming paper surface.
- Waterproof and acid free
- Ink formulas and colors consistent for over 25 years
- Low odor, nontoxic and environmentally friendly
- Works on multiple surfaces
- Refillable
- Replacement and optional nibs available
- Logical color-label system

The Joy of Coloring

Coloring, at first glance, may seem childish, unimportant, silly even—an act that many of us did when we were young. But think back—remember why you colored, and how you felt when you were doing it.

For Marianne and me, coloring is an important aspect of our jobs, but it's much more than that. Coloring is a form of communication, a way to gather the ideas from our heads and transfer them to paper, creating a visual image that is easily understood. Coloring is also a form of relaxation. The act of coloring itself becomes a meditation that relieves stress, relaxes the body and clarifies thought processes. Coloring is something we both love … and we want you to love it too.

With the myriad of coloring mediums that are available, it's easy to feel overwhelmed and even frustrated. Fortunately, Copic brand alcohol ink markers are easy tools to use! With the huge color selection and the clear-cut numbering system, there's no guesswork involved, so you can forget about the "how" and focus on the "do."

With the tips, techniques and projects in this book, we hope to lead you down the road to successful (and frustration-free) coloring … ENJOY!

—*Colleen and Marianne*

Marker Styles

There are four styles of Copic markers to choose from.
Regardless of the style, the quality and ink are the same.

Copic Original
- Square barrel
- Double-ended
- Standard nibs: broad chisel and fine
- 7 other nib options
- Empty markers available
- Nesting caps
- Color code written on each cap
- Airbrush system compatible
- 214 colors

Sketch
- Oval barrel
- Double-ended
- Standard nibs: medium broad chisel and super brush
- 1 other optional nib
- Empty markers available
- Color code written on each cap
- Airbrush system compatible
- 346 colors

Ciao
- Round barrel
- Double-ended
- Standard nibs: medium broad chisel and super brush
- 1 other nib option
- Color code written on the side of each marker
- Nesting caps
- 180 colors

Wide
- Flat barrel
- 21mm angled nib standard
- 1 other nib option
- Empty markers available
- Cap nests
- Color code written on cap
- 36 colors

The Secret Code

Understanding the Copic Color System

These markers blend beautifully, but you need to be able to pick colors that work well together to get them to blend easily. That's where the secret code comes in. The numbers and letters on the marker represent the three classifications within the Copic Color System.

Broad Classification (Letter)

The letter, or letters, represents the color family. For example:

B—Blue
RV—Red-Violet
Y—Yellow
BG—Blue-Green

Intermediate Classification (First Number)

This is the color saturation. Lower numbers indicate colors that are more pure and vibrant. Higher numbers indicate colors that are less saturated and toned-down.

Specific Classification (Second Number)

This is the color shade. Lower numbers indicate lighter shades and higher numbers indicate darker shades.

R21
Sardonyx

R24
Prawn

R27
Cadmium Red

Blending Rules

Use the following "rules" to pick colors that naturally work together and blend well.

First, match the color letter(s)—keeping the color family the same.

Then match the color saturation number—keeping the tone the same.

Lastly, pick color brightness numbers within 2 or 3 digits from each other. Example: B21, B24, B26.

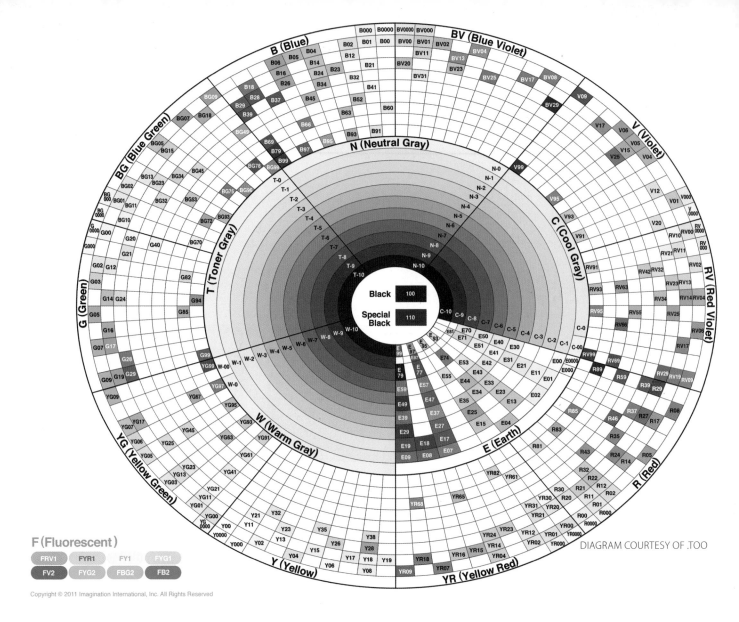

DIAGRAM COURTESY OF .TOO

Copyright © 2011 Imagination International, Inc. All Rights Reserved

Product Compatibility

To get the best results from your Copic markers, it's vital to use the right inks and papers. While we recommend X-Press It Blending Card and Memento Dye Inks—and many of the samples in this book were created using those—it's important to do your own testing for product compatibility as everyone's inking and coloring styles are different. It's often a matter of personal preference.

Testing Inks

Stamp image onto the paper; let dry completely. Scribble over the stamped image with the Colorless Blender. Does the stamped ink bleed or feather? If yes—it's not a compatible ink. If no—then it's a good ink to use with your Copic markers.

Testing Papers

Draw a circle with a pencil or compatible inking pen. Color up to the edges using a lot of ink, saturating your paper. Does the ink feather outside the lines? If yes—the paper may not be compatible. If no— then it's a good paper for your Copic marker use.

Testing Digital Images

Print your images as normal and test the printer ink in the same way you would stamping ink. If your printer ink isn't compatible, you can heat-set the image or make a laser copy before coloring.

For more product information, please visit www.copicmarker.com.

Inking Techniques

There are various ways to add ink to paper. The two most common ways are circling and flicking. Each technique produces a particular appearance, and knowing how to utilize them will add depth and variation to your creations.

Smooth Coloring

Copic makers have the unique ability to lay down smooth, even color without streaks. Using the following steps, practice smooth coloring with a variety of colors and shades until you achieve a smooth image every time.

Do not color with back-and-forth strokes as this will not saturate the paper evenly and will leave you with streaks.

Step 1: Color in small circles. This will keep the leading edge "wet" and allow the ink to blend with itself, creating a seamless look.

Step 2: Make sure to saturate the entire area so that you eliminate any light or mottled areas.

Step 3: Check the back of your paper to make sure that the ink is saturating though evenly.

Tips & Troubleshooting

• *Letting an area dry and going back over it will create uneven patches.*

• *Over-saturating or using too much ink may make your ink feather outside the image.*

Stamp image from
Our Craft Lounge

> Flicks can be left unblended to create texture or they can be blended out to create smooth shading.

Stamp image from Stampavie

Flicking

This technique is achieved by applying ink in quick, single strokes. The key to this inking technique is to "flick" the marker tip across the paper to create a single stroke that goes from dark to light.

Step 1: Holding the marker loosely, start a downward movement toward the paper.

Step 2: As the marker tip touches the paper, quickly move across the paper, bringing your hand up and away at the end of the stroke. This will apply more ink at the beginning of the stroke and less ink at the end.

Tips & Troubleshooting

• *Flick with the side of the nib for larger, smoother strokes or use the tip of the nib for narrow strokes.*

• *If you are getting a blob of ink at the beginning of your stroke, make sure to start moving your marker as soon as it touches the paper. The longer it sits in one spot, the more ink the paper will absorb.*

• *If you are getting a curved "c" or "u" shape instead of a straight line, you might be moving your arm instead of your wrist/fingers.*

Blending
Techniques

One of the most exciting aspects of Copic markers is their blending capability. On the following pages are some basic techniques for coloring and blending that range from using a single color to using multiple shades of each color.

One-Color Shading

Many crafters just are just starting to collect Copic markers and don't have full blending groups. That's OK! You can still create subtle shading with just one marker.

Tips & Troubleshooting

- *If you want the edges blended, use the flicking method to apply the secondary layers of ink.*

Step 1: Lay down a smooth base coat of ink.

Step 2: Let the area dry completely.

If the ink blends instead of darkening, the first layer may not be completely dry.

Step 3: Go over the area you want shaded with the same color. By adding another layer of the same color over itself, you can create a darker shade of that color.

Step 4: Repeat steps 2 and 3 as necessary.

Stamp image from Stamping Bella

Tip-to-Tip Transferring

One of the unique qualities of Copic markers is that ink can be transferred from one marker tip to another without contaminating the color or ruining the nibs.

• Control the amount of ink applied for the best contrast and blending.

Too much orange on the tip.

Not enough orange on the tip.

Just right!

Step 1: Hold the lighter marker horizontally. Hold the darker marker with the tip pointed down. Touch the two tips together and hold for a few seconds.

Step 2: Dark ink is transferred to the tip of the lighter marker.

The Tip-to-Tip method transfers a bit less ink and is therefore a more subtle effect. For a more dramatic blend, use the Palette Transferring method.

Step 3: Apply ink to your image either by scribbling in small circles or flicking. The darker ink will be applied first. As you continue coloring, the lighter ink will be applied and blend the two colors together.

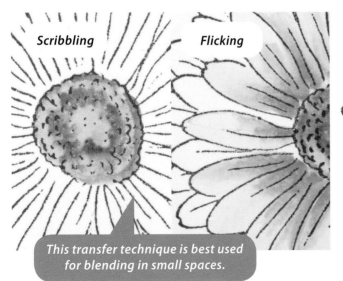

Scribbling

Flicking

This transfer technique is best used for blending in small spaces.

Step 4: Repeat steps 1–3 as often as necessary.

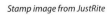

Stamp image from JustRite

Palette Transferring

This transfer technique uses a lighter marker to pick up darker ink from a palette as with a paintbrush.

> You should see the darker ink on the lighter-marker nib.

> If you lose all of the dark color, you are over-blending with the light ink.

Step 1: Scribble darker-color ink onto a nonporous surface. An acrylic stamp block works great for this.

Step 2: Using a lighter-color marker, pick up the darker ink from the palette.

Tips & Troubleshooting

• *Both techniques can be used with the colorless blender to blend from a color to white.*

• *If you have a larger area and want to add shading with this method, apply a smooth base coat of light-color ink first and then add shading with the transfer method.*

Step 3: Apply ink to your image using the same strokes as the Tip-to-Tip method.

Feathering

This challenging blending technique blends two different colors together seamlessly.

> This technique is difficult and takes practice—don't get discouraged if your blends aren't smooth at first.

> It is important to have enough area where the two colors meet that they overlap. Make sure to start your ink application far enough apart for this.

Step 1: Begin with two markers from different color families.

Tips & Troubleshooting

• *It's much easier to blend colors from families next to or near each other on the color wheel. It is more difficult to blend colors that are complementary (or opposite each other on the color wheel).*

• *The lighter the shade, the easier to blend. Darker shades require much more work to blend smoothly.*

• *This technique is wonderful for flower petals, clothing or landscapes where you want a change not in shade, but in color.*

Step 2: Begin flicking the lighter ink onto your image. Try to get smooth, wide strokes by using the side of the nib.

> The flicked strokes need to follow the direction of the shape.

Step 3: Flick the darker ink onto your image coming from the opposite direction. The inks should overlap in the center.

Step 4: You may not get a smooth blend the first time. If not, repeat steps 2 and 3 to saturate and blend smoothly.

Stamp image from Hero Arts

On-Paper Blending

This is the most common blending technique and uses not two, but three or more shades to create highlights and shading.

Step 1: Pick three markers that form a good blending group—a light, a medium and a dark.

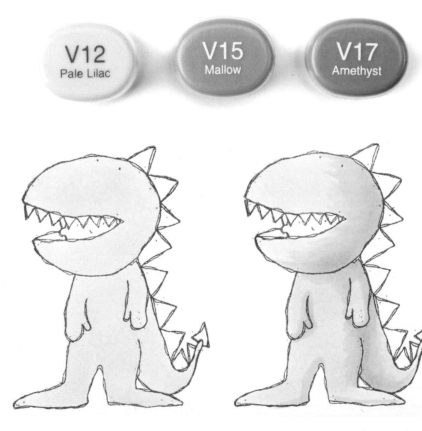

Step 2: Apply a smooth layer of the lightest-color ink to your image.

Step 3: Apply the medium color to the areas you want shadowed.

Step 4: Use the light color to blend along the area where the two colors meet.

Using the flicking technique to apply secondary layers of ink will help start the blending process and reduce the amount of ink needed for a smooth blend.

Tips & Troubleshooting
- *Remember that wet on wet blends, so color only one part of the image at a time to keep the working area saturated.*

> *Don't over-blend or you will lose contrast. If you do, continue reworking the area by adding darker colors and blending back to light.*

Step 5: Apply the dark color to the areas you want shaded darkest.

Step 6: Use the medium color to blend along the area where the dark and the medium colors meet.

Step 7: Lightly blend any remaining lines with the lightest color.

Stamp image from My Favorite Things

Colorless Blender

The Colorless Blender marker is one you really need in your coloring arsenal. While the blender doesn't actually blend, it can be used for a number of other techniques and effects.

Clarifying the Colorless Blender

What Does the Colorless Blender Do?

As you now know, any lighter-colored marker will move the ink of a darker-colored marker. The Colorless Blender is the lightest of all the markers; it contains no pigment at all and is purely the alcohol solution. Because of this the Colorless Blender will move all other colors. The following compares No Blending, On-Paper Blending and "blending" with the Colorless Blender.

Most people think the blender bleaches out the color, but in reality it just moves it.

No blending

On-Paper Blending

Colorless Blender

Light, medium and dark shades of green are applied to the circle. At this point, they are not blended.

When you blend using the On-Paper Blending technique, which uses the lighter-colored markers to blend the colors together, you get a nice gradation of color.

And here's the same group of three colors "blended" with the Colorless Blender marker. As you can see, the colors didn't blend at all, they lightened and moved around.

Moving Color With the Colorless Blender

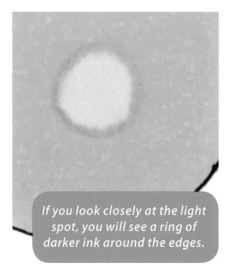

In this sample, the image was colored with a smooth layer of medium green. The Colorless Blender marker was then touched to the surface and held for about five seconds.

As you can see, there is a light spot where the Colorless Blender touched. This is because the green particles reacted with the Colorless Blender and moved away from it—piling up around the edges.

If you look closely at the light spot, you will see a ring of darker ink around the edges.

Colorless Blender Techniques

There are three techniques that use the "movement" properties of the Colorless Blender. These three things are what make this marker indispensible!

Fixing Mistakes

Think of the Colorless Blender as your magic eraser. While it doesn't actually erase ink, it can push it back into a colored image. If you color outside the lines, use the Colorless Blender to "push" the ink back toward the colored image.

Remember that the pigment will form a dark ridge in front of the blender. Don't go all the way up to the line with the blender or you will push the ridge into the colored image making it visible on the other side. Stop just before the line and use the stamped image to "hide" the dark ridge. This does take some practice. Some colors will be easier to move than others.

A favorite use of the blender is for adding texture.

Stamp image from Gina K. Designs

Once the paper is saturated with blender, it won't do any good to keep adding more. If the mistake remains, let the ink dry completely and repeat.

Adding Texture

Touch either the brush or chisel nib of the Colorless Blender to the surface of a colored image. Hold for a few seconds and lift. Notice the shape and size of the lightened area. If you use the Colorless Blender on wet colored images the area will have fuzzy, indistinct edges. If you use it on a dry colored image the edges will be more crisp and distinct.

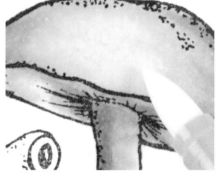

Lightening Color

If an area on your image gets too dark, you can lighten it a bit with the Colorless Blender. Keep in mind that pigment particles will pile up making a dark ridge if the blender marker is left in one spot or used in a back-and-forth motion. Use a flicking motion with the Colorless Blender to avoid this.

thinking of you

apples

Creative
Coloring
Projects

Don't Worry, Be Happy

Design by **Colleen Schaan**

Techniques Used
- On-Paper Blending
- Transfer Blending

Coloring Instructions

1. Stamp fish onto white smooth cardstock.

2. Using On-Paper Blending technique, color fish's body with BG11, BG72 and BG75.

3. Color fins, ears and lips with YR04. Using a Transfer Blending technique, shade with YR07.

Assembly Instructions

Form a 4¼ x 5½-inch top-folded card from white smooth cardstock.

Adhere a 3⅞ x 5⅛-inch piece of light teal Dotted Swiss cardstock to black cardstock; trim a small border. Adhere to card front.

Stamp "don't worry be happy" onto a 3⅞ x 1½-inch piece of white smooth cardstock. Adhere to a 3⅞ x 1⅝-inch piece of black cardstock. Adhere to card front as shown.

Cut out fish. Using foam tape, attach fish to card front as shown.

Using Multiliner, draw a dotted border around edges of light teal and sentiment panels. ❧

Sources: White smooth X-Press It Blending Card, markers and Multiliner from Imagination International Inc.; colored cardstock from Bazzill Basics Paper Inc.; stamp set from Gina K. Designs; Memento dye ink pad from Tsukineko LLC.

Materials
Cardstock: white smooth, light teal
   Dotted Swiss, black
Quite a Catch stamp set
Black dye ink pad
Markers: BG11, BG72, BG75, YR04, YR07
Black Multiliner
Adhesive foam tape
Paper adhesive

Materials

Cardstock: white smooth, blue,
 apple green
Apples in Chintz Bowl stamp
Black dye ink pad
Markers: B21, B23, B26, C-1, E33, YG17,
 YG21, YG23, YG25
Colorless Blender (0)
4¾ inches ⅝-inch-wide apple green
 ribbon
Die templates: Labels One (#S4-161),
 Large Labels (#S4-168)
Victoria embossing folder (#37-1916)
Die-cutting and embossing machine
Sanding block
Adhesive foam tape
Paper adhesive

Apples in a Chintz Bowl

Design by **Sharon Harnist**

Techniques Used

- On-Paper Blending
- One-Color Shading

Coloring Instructions

1. Stamp apples in bowl onto white smooth cardstock.

2. Using On-Paper Blending technique, color apples with YG21, YG23 and YG25.

3. Color stems with E33.

4. Using One-Color Shading technique, color and shade leaves with YG17.

5. Color base of bowl with B21.

6. Use Colorless Blender to remove color from flowers on bowl.

7. Using On-Paper Blending technique, add shadows with B23 and B26.

8. Remove any excess color from white flowers with Colorless Blender.

9. Add shadows under bowl with C-1. Blend it out to white with Colorless Blender.

Assembly Instructions

Form a 5¼ x 4-inch top-folded card from blue cardstock. Using Victoria embossing folder, emboss front and back of card; lightly sand.

Using 3¾ x 2⅞-inch Large Labels die template, die-cut a label from apple green cardstock. Attach to card front using foam tape.

Trim a V-notch into each end of ribbon; attach to card front as shown.

Using 2⅜-inch Labels One die template, die-cut a label from colored image panel. Attach to card front using foam tape. ❧

Sources: *White smooth X-Press It Blending Card, markers and Colorless Blender from Imagination International Inc.; colored cardstock from Memory Box; stamp from Lockhart Stamp Co.; Memento dye ink pad from Tsukineko LLC; die templates from Spellbinders™ Paper Arts; Cuttlebug embossing folder from Provo Craft.*

Joyous Journey

Design by **Lori Craig**

Techniques Used
- Smooth Coloring
- Transfer Blending

Coloring Instructions

1. Using brown dye ink, stamp balloon onto white smooth cardstock.

2. Using Smooth Coloring technique, color outer segments of balloon with BG72. Using a Transfer Blending technique, shade with BG75.

3. In the same manner as first segment, color next two segments of balloon with Y17; shade with Y19.

4. Color two narrow segments of balloon with YG21; shade with YG25.

5. Color center segment of balloon with YR02; shade with YR07.

Assembly Instructions

Form a 4¼ x 5½-inch top-folded card from light yellow cardstock. Adhere a 3½ x 1-inch piece of Picnic Fun paper and a 3⅓ x 3¾-inch piece of Blue Sky paper to a 3⅝ x 4⅞-inch piece of dark brown cardstock, as shown. Using brown pearlescent ink, stamp hot-air balloon onto layered panel as shown. Color basket using E31.

Using brown pearlescent ink, stamp sentiment below balloon.

Using Top Note die, die-cut a 3⅝ x ¾-inch strip of turquoise cardstock. Adhere to layered panel as shown.

Wrap twine around layered panel twice; secure ends to back.

Cut out colored balloon. Using foam tape, attach over balloon stamped on layered panel. Attach layered panel to card front using foam tape.

Using Tattered Florals die, die-cut a flower from music sheet paper. Adhere to card front as shown.

Thread twine through button. Tie bow on front; trim ends. Attach to die-cut flower. ❧

Sources: *White smooth X-Press It Blending Card and markers from Imagination International Inc.; colored cardstock from Papertrey Ink; printed papers from Echo Park Paper Co.; stamps from Verve Stamps; Memento dye ink pad and Brilliance pearlescent ink pad from Tsukineko LLC; dies from Sizzix.*

Materials
Cardstock: white smooth, light yellow, dark brown, turquoise
Printed papers: Sweet Summertime Blue Sky, A Walk in the Park Picnic Fun, music sheet
Stamp sets: Up, Up & Away, Joy for the Journey
Ink pads: brown dye, brown pearlescent
Markers: BG72, BG75, E31, Y17, Y19, YG21, YG25, YR02, YR07
Orange button
White twine
Dies: Tattered Florals (#656640), Top Note (#113463)
Die-cutting machine
Adhesive foam tape
Paper adhesive

You Are My Sunshine

Design by **Marianne Walker**

Techniques Used
- Transfer Blending
- Flicking

Coloring Instructions

1. Stamp images onto a piece of white smooth cardstock.

2. Color sun with YR31. Using a Transfer Blending technique, shade with YR16.

3. Using a Transfer Blending technique and Flicking technique, flick YR16 with YR31 onto flower petals.

4. Using a Transfer Blending technique and Flicking technique, flick YG93 with YG03 onto leaves.

5. Add shading to cloud with B41; do not blend.

Assembly Instructions

Form a 3¾ x 4⅞-inch side-folded card from white cardstock. Adhere a 3⅛ x 4½-inch piece of printed paper to card front. Adhere a 2¼ x 3-inch piece of pink cardstock to card front.

Cut out all stamped images. Adhere to card front as shown, using foam tape on cloud and flower.

Stamp "You are my" and "SUNSHINE" onto white smooth cardstock. Cut out sentiments; adhere to card front as shown. ❧

Materials
Cardstock: white smooth, white, pink
Girl Friday Sunday printed paper
Sunshine Cheer stamp set
Black dye ink pad
Markers: B41, YG03, YG93, YR16, YR31
Die templates: Standard Circles SM (#S4-116), Standard Circles LG (#S4-114), Classic Scalloped Circles LG (#S4-124)
Die-cutting and embossing machine
Adhesive foam tape
Paper adhesive

Sources: White smooth X-Press It Blending Card and markers from Imagination International Inc.; printed paper from Cosmo Cricket; stamp set from Our Craft Lounge; Memento dye ink pad from Tsukineko LLC; die templates from Spellbinders™ Paper Arts; die-cutting machine from Sizzix.

Home Sweet Home

Design by Colleen Schaan

Materials

Cardstock: white smooth, black, golden yellow
Love Shack Party double-sided printed paper
Stamps: Swiss Birdhouse digital, Everyday Sayings set
Black dye ink pad
Markers: E11, E18, R43, R46, Y32, Y38, YG17
Black Multiliner
Adhesive foam tape
Paper adhesive
Computer with printer

Techniques Used

- Transfer Blending
- One-Color Shading

Coloring Instructions

1. Print birdhouse onto white smooth cardstock. Cut a 3 x 3-inch square around birdhouse image.

2. Color birdhouse with E11. Using a Transfer Blending technique, shade with E18.

3. Color heart and flowers with R43. Using a Transfer Blending technique, shade with R46.

4. Using One-Color Shading technique, color and shade leaves with YG17.

5. Color butterflies with Y32. Using a Transfer Blending technique, shade with Y38.

Assembly Instructions

Form a 4¼ x 4¼-inch side-folded card from black cardstock. Adhere a 4 x 1¾-inch piece of printed paper to a 4 x 4-inch piece of golden yellow cardstock, aligning bottom edges. Adhere to card front.

Adhere a 4 x 1⅛-inch piece of black cardstock to card front as shown.

Adhere birdhouse panel to black cardstock; trim a small border. Stamp "thank you" onto lower right corner. Using Multiliner, draw a border around edges of panel and card front. Using foam tape, attach birdhouse panel to card front. 🍃

Sources: White smooth X-Press It Blending Card, markers and Multiliner from Imagination International Inc.; colored cardstock from Bazzill Basics Paper Inc.; printed paper from Bo-Bunny Press; digital stamp from C.C. Designs Rubber Stamps; stamp set from Hero Arts; Memento dye ink pad from Tsukineko LLC.

Sew With All Your Heart

Design by **Colleen Schaan**

Techniques Used
- On-Paper Blending
- Transfer Blending
- Flicking

Coloring Instructions

1. Using black ink, stamp heart onto white smooth cardstock.

2. Using On-Paper Blending technique, color heart with R02, R05 and R08.

3. Color leaves with YG63. Using a Transfer Blending technique, shade with YG67.

4. Using a Transfer Blending technique and Flicking technique, flick YR20 with YR24 onto flower petals.

5. Color button with YR68.

6. Using paintbrush, add pinheads with pigment paint. Let dry completely.

Assembly Instructions

Form a 4¼ x 5½-inch top-folded card from rust cardstock.

Adhere a 3½ x 4½-inch piece of plaid paper to yellow cardstock; trim a border. Distress edges of yellow cardstock with bone folder. Adhere a 3½ x 2-inch piece of ruler paper to layered panel. Machine-stitch around panel as shown; adhere to card front.

Adhere lace to card front as shown, gathering lace as desired.

Using 2⅛-inch Standard Circles SM die template, die-cut a circle around colored heart. Distress and ink edges light brown. Cut a 2¼-inch circle from yellow cardstock. Distress and ink edges light brown. Adhere image circle to yellow circle. Machine-stitch around edge as shown.

Slide pearl stickpin through layered circles. Using foam tape, attach to card front. ❧

Sources: *White smooth X-Press It Blending Card, markers and pigment paint from Imagination International Inc.; colored cardstock from Bazzill Basics Paper Inc.; paper pad from Cosmo Cricket; stamp set from JustRite; Memento dye ink pad from Tsukineko LLC; distress dye ink pad from Ranger Industries Inc.; die templates from Spellbinders™ Paper Arts; die-cutting machine from Sizzix.*

Materials
Cardstock: white smooth, rust, yellow
Material Girl Mini Deck paper pad
Stitched with Love Borders & Centers
   stamp set
Dye ink pads: black, light brown distress
Markers: R02, R05, R08, YG63, YG67, YR20,
   YR24, YR68
White pigment paint
5 inches ¾-inch-wide cream lace
Pearl stickpin
Standard Circles SM die templates (#S4-116)
Die-cutting machine
Small paintbrush
Bone folder
Sewing machine with orange thread
Adhesive foam tape
Paper adhesive

Materials

4¼ x 5½-inch black/white note card
Cardstock: white smooth, black, ivory
Grow Bingo Card
Classic Red/Black Paper Pad
My Garden Borders & Centers stamp set
Dye ink pads: black, light brown distress
Markers: R24, R29, R39, T-1, T-3, T-5
9 inches ½-inch-wide red seam binding
Die templates: Standard Circles SM (#S4-116), Standard Circles LG (#S4-114), Petite Scalloped Circles SM (#S4-117), Petite Scalloped Circles LG (#S4-115)
Die-cutting machine
Black glitter glue
Adhesive foam tape
Paper adhesive

Friends Are Flowers

Design by Sharon Harnist

Techniques Used

- Transfer Blending
- Flicking

Coloring Instructions

1. Using black ink, stamp flower onto white smooth cardstock.

2. Color flower petals with R24. Using a Transfer Blending technique, shade with R29.

3. Using Flicking technique, add additional shading by flicking on R39.

4. Color flower center with T-3.

5. Using a Transfer Blending technique, shade with T-5.

6. Using Flicking technique, shade around outside of flower by flicking T-1 from flower outward.

Assembly Instructions

Adhere a 4 x 4-inch piece of butterfly paper and a 4 x 1¼-inch piece of red floral paper to front of note card as shown.

Adhere bingo card to black cardstock; trim a small border. Attach to card front as shown, using foam tape.

Using 2⅛-inch Standard Circles SM die template, die-cut a circle around colored flower. Ink edges light brown.

Using 2¼-inch Petite Scalloped Circles SM die template, die-cut a scalloped circle from black cardstock. Adhere flower circle to scalloped circle.

Using black ink, stamp sentiment circle onto ivory cardstock. Using 3¼-inch Standard Circles LG die template, die-cut a circle around sentiment circle. Ink edges light brown.

Using 3½-inch Petite Scalloped Circle LG die template, die-cut a scalloped circle from black cardstock. Adhere sentiment circle to scalloped circle.

Using foam tape, layer and adhere circles to card front as shown.

Tie a bow with seam binding; trim ends. Adhere to card front as shown. Apply glitter glue to center of flower; let dry completely. ❧

Sources: *Note card from Memory Box; white smooth X-Press It Blending Card and markers from Imagination International Inc.; colored cardstock from Gina K. Designs; bingo card and paper pad from Jenni Bowlin Studio; stamp set from JustRite; Memento dye ink pad from Tsukineko LLC; distress dye ink pad and glitter glue from Ranger Industries Inc.; die templates from Spellbinders™ Paper Arts; die-cutting machine from Sizzix.*

Dancing Queen

Design by **Colleen Schaan**

Techniques Used
- Transfer Blending
- Flicking
- On-Paper Blending

Coloring Instructions

1. Stamp girl onto white smooth cardstock.

2. Color skin with E51. Using a Transfer Blending technique, shade with E53.

3. Using Flicking technique, color hair by flicking with N-2, N-4 and N-6. Leave highlight white and don't blend.

4. Using On-Paper Blending technique, color clothing with R22, R24 and R27.

5. Using On-Paper Blending technique, color shoes and slip with N-2, N-4 and N-6.

6. Color crown with Y18.

Assembly Instructions

Form a 5 x 5-inch top-folded card from black cardstock. Using 4⅛-inch Classic Scalloped Circles LG die template, die-cut card, leaving top-folded edge intact.

Using 2¾-inch Standard Circles LG die template, die-cut circle around stamped girl. Using Multiliner, draw a border around edge of circle.

Using 3-inch Standard Circles SM die template, die-cut a circle from black cardstock. Die-cut a 3½-inch circle from printed paper.

Layer and adhere circles together. Attach to card front using foam tape. ❧

Sources: *White smooth X-Press It Blending Card, markers and Multiliner from Imagination International Inc.; black cardstock from Bazzill Basics Paper Inc.; printed paper from Kaisercraft; Missmatch Ketto stamp from Stamping Bella; stamp set from Hero Arts; Memento dye ink pad from Tsukineko LLC; die templates from Spellbinders™ Paper Arts; die-cutting and embossing machine from Sizzix.*

Materials
Cardstock: white smooth, black
Shaken Not Stirred Roger printed paper
Stamps: Missmatch Ketto, Everyday Sayings set
Black dye ink pad
Markers: E51, E53, N-2, N-4, N-6, R22, R24, R27, Y18
Black Multiliner
Die templates: Standard Circles SM (#S4-116), Standard Circles LG (#S4-114), Classic Scalloped Circles LG (#S4-124)
Die-cutting and embossing machine
Adhesive foam tape
Paper adhesive

Friends Forever

Design by **Michele Boyer**

Techniques Used
- Transfer Blending
- On-Paper Blending
- One-Color Shading
- Flicking

Coloring Instructions

1. Stamp girl onto a 2⅛ x 3⅜-inch piece of cream smooth cardstock.

2. Color face and arms with E000. Using a Transfer Blending technique, shade with E00.

3. Using a Transfer Blending technique, add cheek color by transferring R20 to E000 and tapping lightly on the paper.

4. Color hair with E33. Using a Transfer Blending technique, shade with E35.

5. Using On-Paper Blending technique, color shirt with R81, R83 and R85.

6. Using One-Color Shading technique, color and shade flower with YG93.

7. Using On-Paper Blending technique, color pants with E31, E33 and E35.

8. Using Flicking technique, create shading around image by flicking YG0000 outward from image.

9. Add ground using W-00 and W-1.

Assembly Instructions

Form a 5¼ x 5¼-inch top-folded card from dark brown cardstock.

Cut a 4¾ x 4¾-inch piece from Doilies paper. Adhere a 4⅜ x 3⅞-inch piece of Slipcover paper to dark brown cardstock; trim a small border. Adhere to Doilies panel as shown.

Cut a 2¼ x 4⅜-inch piece from Slipcover paper. Adhere to dark brown cardstock; trim a small border. Adhere to Doilies panel as shown.

Zigzag-stitch edges of printed paper panels as desired. Wrap ribbon around left edge of layered Doilies panel; secure left end to back. Allow right end of ribbon to extend past right edge of printed paper panel; trim end. Wrap lace around Doilies panel in the same manner.

Stamp "Friends Forever" onto layered panel as shown. Sprinkle with embossing powder; heat-emboss.

Adhere girl panel to dark brown cardstock; trim a small border. Adhere to Doilies panel, zigzag-stitch along top left and bottom right corners.

Materials
Cardstock: cream smooth, dark brown
Restoration Collection double-sided printed papers: Doilies, Slipcover
Felt: green, brown
Stamp sets: Being Cute Is What I Do, A Cart Full of Friends
Black dye ink pad
Clear embossing powder
Markers: E000, E00, E31, E33, E35, R20, R81, R83, R85, W-00, W-1, YG0000, YG93
6 inches ⅞-inch-wide brown ribbon
6 inches ⅝-inch-wide cream lace
Rolled Rose die
Die-cutting machine
Embossing heat tool
Sewing machine with white thread
Adhesive foam dots
Paper adhesive

Adhere Doilies layer to dark brown cardstock; trim a small border. Adhere to card front using foam dots.

Using Rolled Rose die, die-cut flower from brown felt. Hand-cut two leaves from green felt. Roll die-cut flower; adhere to card front as shown. Adhere leaves tucked behind flower as shown. ❧

Sources: *Cream smooth cardstock, felt, stamp sets and die from My Favorite Things; brown cardstock from Papertrey Ink; printed papers from Crate Paper Inc.; Memento dye ink pad from Tsukineko LLC; markers from Imagination International Inc.*

Kahlua Koala

Design by Colleen Schaan

Techniques Used
- On-Paper Blending
- Transfer Blending

Coloring Instructions

1. Stamp koala and tree onto a 3 x 3¼-inch piece of white smooth cardstock.

2. Using On-Paper Blending technique, color body with W-1, W-3 and W-5.

3. Color nose with W-3. Using a Transfer Blending technique, shade with W-7.

4. Using On-Paper Blending technique, color tree with E13, E25 and E27.

5. Color leaves with YG41. Using a Transfer Blending technique, shade with YG45.

Assembly Instructions

Form a 4¼ x 5½-inch side-folded card from light green cardstock.

Adhere a 3⅞ x 5⅛-inch piece of green cardstock to black cardstock; trim a small border. Adhere to card front.

Adhere a 3⅞ x 3-inch piece of printed paper to black cardstock; trim a small border. Adhere to card front as shown.

Using Multiliner, draw a border around koala/tree panel. Adhere to black cardstock; trim a small border. Adhere to card front.

Thread button with ribbon. Tie knot on front; trim ends. Adhere to upper left corner of image panel. ❧

Sources: White smooth X-Press It Blending Card, markers and Multiliner from Imagination International Inc.; colored cardstock from Bazzill Basics Paper Inc.; stamp from Whipper Snapper Designs Inc.; stamp set from Gina K. Designs; Memento dye ink pad from Tsukineko LLC.

Hang in There!

Materials
Cardstock: white smooth, light green, green, black
Light green printed paper
Stamps: Kahlua, Hang in There set
Black dye ink pad
Markers: E13, E25, E27, W-1, W-3, W-5, W-7, YG41, YG45
Black Multiliner
White button
3⅓ inches ¼-inch-wide light green grosgrain ribbon
Adhesive foam tape
Paper adhesive

Potted Plant

Design by **Colleen Schaan**

Materials

Cardstock: white smooth, dark brown, light green, sage green
Origins Aloe printed paper
Seeds of Kindness stamp set
Dye ink pads: black, brown
Markers: C-0, C-2, C-4, C-6, G20, G21, G24, G28
Brown Multiliner
12 inches ⅝-inch-wide hemp twine ribbon
Adhesive foam tape
Paper adhesive

Techniques Used

- Flicking
- On-Paper Blending

Coloring Instructions

1. Using black ink, stamp potted plant onto a 2½ x 4½-inch piece of white smooth cardstock.

2. Color leaves with G20.

3. Using Flicking technique, flick G21 and G24 from center to outsides of leaves using side of nib.

4. Using Flicking technique, flick G28 from center toward outsides of leaves using tip of nib. Do not blend.

5. Using On-Paper Blending technique, color pot with C-0, C-2, C-4 and C-6.

Assembly Instructions

Form a 4¼ x 5½-inch top-folded card from dark brown cardstock.

Cut a 4 x 5¼-inch piece from light green cardstock. Adhere a 3⅞ x 5-inch piece of sage green cardstock to light green piece, and a 3⅞ x 4-inch piece of printed paper to sage green panel as shown. Cut a 4 x 1⅝-inch piece from dark brown cardstock; adhere to layered panel, 2⅝ inches below top edge.

Wrap ribbon around layered panel over dark brown piece. Tie knot on right side; trim ends.

Adhere potted plant panel to dark brown cardstock; trim a small border. Using Multiliner, draw a border around edge of panel.

Using brown ink, stamp sentiment onto white smooth cardstock. Cut a rectangle around sentiment; using Multiliner, draw a border around edge of rectangle. Adhere rectangle to dark brown cardstock; trim a small border. Adhere to potted plant panel as shown. Attach to card front using foam tape. ❧

Sources: White smooth X-Press It Blending Card, markers and Multiliner from Imagination International Inc.; colored cardstock and stamp set from Gina K. Designs; printed paper from BasicGrey; Memento dye ink pads from Tsukineko LLC.

Cupcake Day

Design by Sharon Harnist

Materials

Cardstock: white smooth, white
Oliver printed papers: Charlie, Keagan, Mason
Stamps: Single Cupcake, Happy Cupcake Day
Black dye ink pad
Markers: BG11, BG72, E31, E33, E35, R37, R39, T-1, T-2
Clear glitter pen
9 inches ¼-inch-wide green grosgrain ribbon
Punches: Traditional Scallop Edge, corner rounder
Die templates: Standard Circles LG (#S4-114), Petite Scalloped Circles SM (#S4-117), Ribbon Tags Trio (#S3-150)
Die-cutting and embossing machine
Airbrush system
Sewing machine with white thread
Scoring tool
Adhesive foam tape
Paper adhesive

Techniques Used

- On-Paper Blending
- Transfer Blending

Coloring Instructions

1. Stamp cupcake onto white smooth cardstock.

2. Using On-Paper Blending technique, color cupcake liner with E31, E33 and E35.

3. Color frosting with BG11. Using a Transfer Blending technique, shade with BG72.

4. Color cherry with R37. Using a Transfer Blending technique, shade with R39.

5. Add shadows with T-1 and T-2.

6. Add glitter to cherry with clear glitter pen.

Assembly Instructions

Form a 5½ x 4¼-inch top-folded card from white cardstock.

Cut a 5½ x 4¼-inch piece from Keagan paper.

Cut a 5½ x 2-inch piece from Charlie paper. Using scallop edge punch, punch bottom edge of Charlie piece. Score a line ½ inch above scalloped edge.

Adhere to Keagan panel as shown so scalloped edge hangs free. Machine-stitch ⅛ inch above scored line.

Stamp "happy cupcake day" onto white cardstock. Using 2¾ x ¾-inch tag die template, die-cut sentiment. Airbrush tag while still in die template using T-1. Remove from template.

Thread a 7-inch length of ribbon through sentiment tag; wrap around Keagan panel along paper seam. Secure ends to back. Tie a knot with remaining ribbon; trim ends and adhere over left edge of sentiment tag. Adhere panel to card front. Round top corners using corner rounder.

Using 1⅞-inch circle die template, die-cut cupcake image. In the same manner as before, airbrush edge of cupcake circle.

Using 2¼-inch scalloped circle die template, die-cut a scalloped circle from Mason paper. Adhere cupcake circle to Mason circle. Attach to card front as shown, using foam tape. ✤

Sources: *White smooth X-Press It Blending Card, markers, clear glitter pen and airbrush system from Imagination International Inc.; white cardstock from Gina K. Designs; printed paper from BasicGrey; stamps from Lockhart Stamp Co.; Memento dye ink pad from Tsukineko LLC; edge punch from Martha Stewart Crafts; die templates from Spellbinders™ Paper Arts.*

Happy Hummingbird

Design by **Colleen Schaan**

Techniques Used
- On-Paper Blending
- Transfer Blending

Coloring Instructions

1. Stamp hummingbird and flowers onto a 3½ x 4¾-inch piece of white smooth cardstock.

2. Using On-Paper Blending technique, color bird with B000, B00 and B02.

3. Color leaves with YG21. Using a Transfer Blending technique, shade with YG25.

4. Color flowers with R81. Using a Transfer Blending technique, shade with R85. Add R89 to flower centers.

5. Color beak with Y19.

6. Add white highlights to flower centers using paintbrush and pigment paint.

Assembly Instructions

Form a 4¼ x 5½-inch top-folded card from light green cardstock. Cut a 4 x 5¼-inch piece from printed paper.

Stamp "thinking of you" along bottom edge of hummingbird panel. Using Multiliner, draw a border around edge of hummingbird panel. Adhere to printed paper panel.

Wrap a 3-inch length of ribbon around top left corner of layered panel; secure ends to back. Tie a bow with remaining ribbon; trim ends. Adhere to ribbon wrapped around layered panel. Adhere to card front. ❧

Sources: *White smooth X-Press It Blending Card, markers, Multiliner and pigment paint from Imagination International Inc.; light green cardstock from Bazzill Basics Paper Inc.; Enchanting Meadows printed paper from KI Memories; Hailey Hummingbird stamp from Whipper Snapper Designs Inc.; Everyday Sayings stamp set from Hero Arts; Memento dye ink pad from Tsukineko LLC.*

Materials

Cardstock: white smooth, light green
Enchanting Meadow printed cardstock
Stamps: Hailey Hummingbird, Everyday
    Sayings set
Black dye ink pad
Markers: B000, B00, B02, R81, R85, R89,
    Y19, YG21, YG25
Black Multiliner
White pigment paint
10 inches ⁷⁄₁₆-inch-wide green ribbon
Small paintbrush
Paper adhesive

Monster Party

Design by **Colleen Schaan**

Materials

Cardstock: white smooth, light blue Dotted Swiss, dark blue Dotted Swiss
Stamps: Monstah Bash, Birthday Balloon Jolinne set
Black dye ink pad
Markers: B93, B95, B97, E41, E43, E93, E95, E97, E99, R02, Y21, Y26
Black Multiliner
White pigment paint
Small paintbrush
Paper adhesive

Techniques Used

- On-Paper Blending
- Transfer Blending

Coloring Instructions

1. Stamp monsters onto a 4 x 2⅝-inch piece of white smooth cardstock.

2. Using On-Paper Blending technique, color middle monster with B93, B95 and B97.

3. Add cheeks with R02.

4. Color horns and feet with E93. Using a Transfer Blending technique, shade with E97.

5. Using On-Paper Blending technique, color right monster with E95, E97 and E99; do not blend fur above eyes.

6. Color left monster with E41. Using a Transfer Blending technique, shade with E43.

7. Color balloon with Y21. Using a Transfer Blending technique, shade with Y26.

8. Using paintbrush, add pigment paint to teeth and spots; let dry completely.

Assembly Instructions

Form a 4 x 5½-inch side-folded card from white smooth cardstock. Adhere a 4 x 4-inch piece of light blue Dotted Swiss cardstock to card front.

Adhere monsters panel to a 4 x 2⅞-inch piece of dark blue Dotted Swiss cardstock. Adhere to card front.

Using Multiliner, draw borders on card as shown. Stamp "Very Happy Birthday" onto upper right corner of light blue panel. ❧

Sources: *White smooth X-Press It Blending Card, markers, Multiliner and pigment paint from Imagination International Inc.; Dotted Swiss cardstock from Bazzill Basics Paper Inc.; Birthday Balloon Jolinne stamp set from My Favorite Things; Monstah Bash stamp from Stamping Bella; Memento dye ink pad from Tsukineko LLC.*

Materials

Cardstock: white smooth, pink
Stamps: butterfly, All Occasion Messages
   stamp set
Black dye ink pad
Markers: BV20, BV23, BV25, R81, R83, R85
Black Multiliner
White pigment paint
20 inches ¹³⁄₁₆-inch-wide white decorative
   ribbon
Charlotte vintage button
Silver craft wire
1¼-inch circle punch
Standard Circles SM die templates (#S4-116)
Medallions, Frame & Damask Embossing
   Folder Set (#656151)
Die-cutting and embossing machine
Small paintbrush
Paper adhesive

Patchwork Butterfly

Design by Colleen Schaan

Techniques Used
- Feathering
- Flicking

Coloring Instructions

1. Stamp butterfly onto white smooth cardstock.

2. Using Feathering technique, color upper wings R81 into BV20.

3. Using Flicking technique, use wide flicks to shade wing tips with R83 and R85 and inner wings with BV23 and BV25.

4. Use R81 and BV20 to blend shading, keeping blend from pink to purple smooth and light.

5. Rotate color location for bottom wings and follow the same steps.

6. Using a small paintbrush, add spots of white to wing details with pigment paint.

Assembly Instructions

Form a 4¼ x 5½-inch top-folded card from white smooth cardstock. Using Damask embossing folder, emboss pattern onto card front.

Cut a 4¼ x 2-inch piece from pink cardstock. Wrap a 6-inch length of ribbon around pink piece; secure ends to back. Adhere to card front as shown.

Using desired Standard Circles SM die template, die-cut circle around butterfly image. Adhere to card front as shown.

Stamp sentiment onto white smooth cardstock. Using circle punch, punch out sentiment. Adhere to card front overlapping bottom left edge of butterfly. Add a border along edge of each circle with Multiliner.

Tie a double bow with remaining ribbon. Attach button to center of bow with a small piece of craft wire. Adhere to left side of card front as shown. ❧

Sources: White smooth X-Press It Blending Card, markers, Multiliner and pigment paint from Imagination International Inc.; pink cardstock and button from Bazzill Basics Paper Inc.; stamp set from Hero Arts; Memento dye ink pad from Tsukineko LLC; die templates from Spellbinders™ Paper Arts; embossing folder set and die-cutting and embossing machine from Sizzix.

To the Moon & Back

Design by **Sherrie Siemens**

Techniques Used
- On-Paper Blending
- Transfer Blending

Coloring Instructions

1. Using black ink, stamp girl in bed onto a 3⅞ x 2⅜-inch piece of white smooth cardstock.

2. Using On-Paper Blending technique, color skin with E50, E21 and E33.

3. Dot R20 for cheeks.

4. Using On-Paper Blending technique, color sheets and shirt with YG01, YG03, G21 and G24.

5. Create a cast shadow for book with G28.

6. Using On-Paper Blending technique, color pillow with R02, R05, R24 and R29. Use Colorless Blender to pull color from right edge of pillow.

7. Color headboard posts, tabletop, and right side of book with R02. This will give the browns a warm under-glow.

8. Using On-Paper Blending technique, color headboard, table and book with E11, E15, E25 and E57.

9. Color hair with E21. Using a Transfer Blending technique, shade with E25.

10. Using On-Paper Blending technique, color lampshade with Y11, Y15 and Y17. Use Colorless Blender to pull color from center of lampshade.

Assembly Instructions

Form a 5½ x 4¼-inch top-folded card from dark brown cardstock. Adhere a 5 x 3¾-inch piece of green printed paper to card front. Using brown ink, stamp sentiment onto upper right corner of green printed paper panel. Wrap ribbon around card front, tie knot on left edge; trim ends.

Adhere image panel to dark brown cardstock; trim a small border. Adhere to card front.

Attach felt stickers to card front as shown. Embellish with gems as desired. ✎♣

Sources: *White smooth X-Press It Blending Card, markers and Colorless Blender from Imagination International Inc.; dark brown cardstock and stamp set from My Favorite Things; Material Girl Mini Deck paper pad from Cosmo Cricket; felt stickers from Martha Stewart Crafts; Memento black dye ink pad from Tsukineko LLC; brown dye ink pad from Ranger Industries Inc.*

Materials
Cardstock: white smooth, dark brown
Material Girl Mini Deck paper pad
White Felt Appliqué Stickers: moon, small star, medium star
Bedtime Story stamp set
Dye ink pads: black, brown
Markers: E11, E15, E21, E25, E33, E50, E57, G21, G24, G28, R02, R05, R20, R24, R29, Y11, Y15, Y17, YG01, YG03
Colorless Blender (0)
Lime green self-adhesive gems
14 inches ⅝-inch-wide brown satin ribbon
Adhesive foam tape
Paper adhesive

Materials

Cardstock: white smooth, kraft
Double-sided printed papers: A Walk in
    the Park Tree Tops, Sweet Summertime
    Summer Argyle
Daisy stamp
Brown dye ink pad
Markers: B91, B93, E00, E31, E51, R00, R22,
    R35, YG21, YG23, YR07, YR21, YR24
3 pink buttons
7 lime green extra-small self-adhesive
    gems
Top Note die (#113463)
Die-cutting machine
5 inches ⅜-inch-wide white crochet trim
White thread
Sewing machine with light brown thread
Adhesive foam tape
Paper adhesive

Daisy

Design by **Lori Craig**

Techniques Used

- Transfer Blending
- Flicking
- On-Paper Blending
- Smooth Coloring

Coloring Instructions

1. Stamp girl on white smooth cardstock.

2. Color skin with E00. Using a Transfer Blending technique, shade with E51.

3. Color hair with YR21. Using a Transfer Blending technique and Flicking technique, shade with flicks of YR24; do not blend.

4. Using On-Paper Blending technique, color flower petals with R00, R22 and R35; blend lightly.

5. Color jeans with B91. Using a Transfer Blending technique, shade with flicks of B93.

6. Using Smooth Coloring technique, color belt with E31, hearts with R35 and patch with YR07.

7. Color shirt and leaves with YG21. Using a Transfer Blending technique, shade with YG23.

8. Using Flicking technique, add flicks of YG21 and YG23 to grass; do not blend.

Assembly Instructions

Form a 4½ x 5½-inch top-folded card from kraft cardstock.

Cut a 3⅞ x 5⅛-inch piece from Tree Tops paper. Adhere to kraft cardstock; trim a small border. Machine-stitch around Tree Tops panel. Adhere to card front.

Adhere a 4½ x 1½-inch piece of Summer Argyle paper below stamped image as shown. Using

Top Note die, die-cut image. Trim around dotted border on die-cut piece. Die-cut another piece using kraft cardstock. Layer and adhere die-cut pieces together. Wrap crochet trim around layered shape as shown. Secure ends to back.

Thread buttons with white thread; tie knots on back, trim ends. Adhere to layered die cuts as shown. Using foam tape, attach to card front. ❧

Sources: *White smooth X-Press It Blending Card and markers from Imagination International Inc.; kraft cardstock from Papertrey Ink; printed papers from Echo Park Paper Co.; stamp from Elisabeth Bell Designs; Memento dye ink pad from Tsukineko LLC; die and die-cutting machine from Sizzix.*

Materials
Cardstock: white smooth, black, purple
  Dotted Swiss
Striped printed paper
Stamps: Lean on Me, Hang in There set
Black dye ink pad
Markers: G20, G24, G28, N-0, N-2, N-4, N-6,
  R81, R85, V12, V15, V17, Y08, YR18
Colorless Blender refill (0)
Black Multiliner
Stipple brush
Paper towel
Paper adhesive

I've Got Your Back

Design by **Colleen Schaan**

Techniques Used

- On-Paper Blending
- Transfer Blending
- Flicking

Coloring Instructions

1. Stamp bear and bunny onto a 5¼ x 2⅜-inch piece of white smooth cardstock.

2. Using On-Paper Blending technique, color bear with N-0, N-2, N-4 and N-6.

3. Using On-Paper Blending technique, color bunny with V12, V15 and V17.

4. Color bunny nose with R81. Using a Transfer Blending technique, shade with R85.

5. Using a Transfer Blending technique and Flicking technique, flick Y08 and YR18 onto butterfly wings.

6. Dip stipple brush into Colorless Blender refill solution; wipe off excess on a paper towel. Tap stipple brush onto colored image to create the look of fur.

7. Color ground with G20. Add dots with G24 and G28 for shading; do not blend.

Assembly Instructions

Form a 5½ x 4¼-inch top-folded card from black cardstock. Adhere a 5¼ x 4-inch piece of purple Dotted Swiss cardstock to card front.

Cut a 5¼ x 2-inch piece from striped paper. Adhere to card front, aligning bottom edge with bottom edge of purple panel.

Using black ink, stamp sentiment onto upper left corner of image panel. Using Multiliner, draw a border around image panel as shown. Adhere to a 5¼ x 2½-inch piece of black cardstock; adhere to card front. ❧

Sources: *White smooth X-Press It Blending Card, markers, Colorless Blender refill and Multiliner from Imagination International Inc.; colored cardstock from Bazzill Basics Paper Inc.; printed paper from Glitz Design; Lean on Me stamp from Whipper Snapper Designs Inc.; Hang in There stamp set from Gina K. Designs; Memento dye ink pad from Tsukineko LLC.*

Layered Flowers

Design by **Colleen Schaan**

Techniques Used
- Feathering
- Smooth Coloring
- Transfer Blending

Coloring Instructions

1. Using black ink, stamp three large flowers and five small flowers onto white smooth cardstock.

2. Using Feathering technique, color petals on large flowers with B12 and B63.

3. Using Smooth Coloring technique, color flower centers and petal tips on small flowers with B12; color small flower petals with B63.

4. Color leaves with G14. Using a Transfer Blending technique, shade with G24.

5. Using paintbrush, add pigment paint to flower centers.

Assembly Instructions

Form a 4¼ x 5½-inch top-folded card from white smooth cardstock.

Adhere a 4¼ x 2½-inch piece of purple cardstock to a 4¼ x 2⅝-inch piece of dark blue cardstock. Adhere to card front as shown. Attach strip of pearls below layered cardstock panel.

Using purple ink, stamp sentiment onto card front as shown.

Cut out all stamped flowers. Adhere flowers to card front as shown, using foam tape on three small flowers. ❧

Sources: White smooth X-Press It Blending Card, markers and pigment paint from Imagination International Inc.; colored cardstock from Bazzill Basics Papers Inc.; Flowering Gems stamp set from Layers of Color; Lean on Me stamp set from Gina K. Designs; Memento dye ink pads from Tsukineko LLC; self-adhesive pearl strip from Kaisercraft.

Materials
Cardstock: white smooth, purple, dark blue
Stamp sets: Flowering Gems, Lean on Me
Dye ink pads: black, purple
Markers: B12, B63, G14, G24
White pigment paint
White self-adhesive pearl strip
Small paintbrush
Adhesive foam tape
Paper adhesive

Pink Peonies

Design by **Sharon Harnist**

Materials

Cardstock: white smooth, dark pink
Sweetness Petite Paper Pad
Beautiful Blossoms Borders & Centers
   stamp set
Brown dye ink pad
Markers: BG0000, BG000, BG10, G21, G24,
   G28, R20, R81, R83, R85, W-3, Y23, Y26
Colorless Blender (0)
Gold glitter pen
7 inches ½-inch-wide yellow seam binding
Apron Lace Border punch
Die templates: Classic Ovals LG (#S4-110),
   Classic Ovals SM (#S4-112)
Die-cutting and embossing machine
Paper distresser
Adhesive foam tape
Paper adhesive

Techniques Used

- On-Paper Blending
- Transfer Blending
- Flicking

Coloring Instructions

1. Stamp peonies and oval frame onto white smooth cardstock.

2. Using On-Paper Blending technique, color peonies with R20, R81, R83 and R85; blend lightly.

3. Using On-Paper Blending technique, color leaves with G21, G24 and G28; blend lightly.

4. Color bow with Y23. Using a Transfer Blending technique, shade with Y26.

5. Add cast shadows with W-3.

6. Using Flicking technique, use flicks to add BG10 to background. Flick from image outward.

7. Using BG000, BG0000 and Colorless Blender, blend from outside of image outward to create a background that fades to white.

8. Add touches of gold glitter pen to bow.

Assembly Instructions

Form a 5½ x 4¼-inch top-folded card from dark pink cardstock. Punch bottom edge of a 5½ x 1¾-inch piece of dark pink cardstock. Adhere to bottom edge of card front.

Cut a 5¼ x 4-inch piece from printed paper; distress edges. Adhere to card front. Cut a ½ x 4-inch strip from decorative edge of printed paper; trim along scalloped pattern on paper. Distress both short edges of strip. Adhere to right edge of printed paper panel.

Cut a V-notch at each end of seam binding. Adhere to card front as shown, gathering as desired while adhering.

Using 2¼ x 3-inch Classic Ovals LG die template, die-cut an oval around peonies. Using 2½ x 3¼-inch Classic Ovals SM die template, die-cut an oval from dark pink cardstock. Layer and adhere ovals together as shown. Attach to card front over gathered seam binding using foam tape. ❧

Sources: *White smooth X-Press It Blending Card, markers, Colorless Blender and glitter pen from Imagination International Inc.; dark pink cardstock from Memory Box; paper pad from Pink Paislee; stamp set from JustRite; Memento dye ink pad from Tsukineko LLC; punch from Fiskars; die templates from Spellbinders™ Paper Arts.*

Key to My Heart

Design by **Colleen Schaan**

Techniques Used

- Flicking
- On-Paper Blending
- Feathering

Coloring Instructions

1. Print girl image onto white smooth cardstock.

2. Color skin with E01. Using Flicking technique, use small flicks from hairline toward center; shade with E21.

3. Using On-Paper Blending technique, color hair with E31, E35 and E37. Add a few dark streaks from crown to tips; do not blend.

4. Using Feathering technique, feather R81 and R85 together for dress. **Note:** *Coloring the whole dress with R81 will help create a smoother blend with less ink. Also, shorten the flicks with the darker color as you add more layers.*

5. Color key and locket with Y18.

Assembly Instructions

Form a 4½ x 4½-inch top-folded card from pink cardstock.

Adhere a 3¾ x 3¾-inch piece of printed paper to bright pink cardstock; trim a border. Adhere to card front.

Stamp sentiment onto white smooth cardstock. Punch sentiment out using 1¼-inch circle punch.

Using 1⅜-inch Standard Circles LG die template, die-cut a circle from bright pink cardstock. Die-cut a 2⅜-inch circle from white cardstock and a 2¾-inch circle from bright pink cardstock.

Adhere sentiment circle to 1⅜-inch bright pink circle. Layer and adhere remaining circles to card front as shown. Adhere sentiment circle to card front overlapping lower left edge of large circle.

Attach gem scroll to card front as shown.

Cut out image. Using foam tape, attach to card front as shown. ✀

Sources: *White smooth X-Press It Blending Card and markers from Imagination International Inc.; colored cardstock from Bazzill Basics Paper Inc.; Key to My Heart digital stamp from Tiddly Inks; Romantic Sentiments Centers stamp set from JustRite; Memento dye ink pad from Tsukineko LLC; self-adhesive gem scroll from Zva Creative; die templates from Spellbinders™ Paper Arts; die-cutting machine from Sizzix.*

Materials

Cardstock: white smooth, pink, bright pink
Pink printed paper
Stamps: Key to My Heart digital, Romantic Sentiments Centers set
Black dye ink pad
Markers: E01, E21, E31, E35, E37, R81, R85, Y18
Self-adhesive gem scroll
1¼-inch circle punch
Standard Circles LG die templates (#S4-114)
Die-cutting machine
Adhesive foam tape
Paper adhesive
Computer with printer

Pretty in Pink

Design by **Debbie Olson**

Techniques Used
- On-Paper Blending
- Transfer Blending

Coloring Instructions

1. Using black ink, stamp flowers onto a piece of white smooth cardstock.

2. Using On-Paper Blending technique, color flowers with R20, R22 and R24.

3. Add darker shading to flowers with R29.

4. Color leaves with G21. Using a Transfer Blending technique, shade with G24 and G28; blend lightly.

5. Fill in space between flowers with YG93.

6. Using On-Paper Blending technique, color pot with E41, E43 and E47.

7. Add cast shadows with C-1, C-3 and C-5.

8. Add additional highlights with Y21.

9. Add a cast shadow for flowers and pot with BV000 and BV02, blending it from darkest near image out to white with Colorless Blender.

10. Place seam binding in a sandwich bag and add several drops of R22 ink refill. Squeeze bag to ink seam binding thoroughly. Remove from bag; let dry.

Assembly Instructions

Form a 4¼ x 5½-inch side-folded card from cream cardstock.

Cut a 4 x 5¼-inch piece from Complete Set paper. Adhere to pink cardstock; trim a small border.

Adhere a 4 x 2⅜-inch piece of One-of-a-Kind paper to a 4 x 2½-inch piece of pink cardstock. Adhere to Complete Set panel as shown. Zigzag-stitch along top and bottom edges of One-of-a-Kind piece.

Wrap dyed seam binding around layered panel as shown; tie bow 1¾ inches above bottom edge. Trim ends of ribbon. Adhere panel to card front.

Using 2¾-inch Standard Circles LG die template, die-cut and emboss a circle around flower image ; ink edges light brown. Using 3-inch Petite Scalloped Circles LG die template, die-cut a scalloped circle from pink cardstock. Layer and adhere circles together. Attach to card front as shown, using foam tape. ❧

Sources: *White smooth X-Press It Blending Card, markers, ink refill and Colorless Blender from Imagination International Inc.; colored cardstock and distress ink pad from Papertrey Ink; printed paper from October Afternoon; stamp from Lockhart Stamp Co.; Memento black dye ink pad from Tsukineko LLC; light brown distress dye ink pad from Ranger Industries Inc.; die templates from Spellbinders™ Paper Arts.*

Materials

Cardstock: white smooth, cream, pink
The Thrift Shop printed papers: Complete Set, One-of-a-Kind
Peonies stamp
Dye ink pads: black, light brown distress
Markers: BV000, BV02, C-1, C-3 C-5, E41, E43, E47, G21, G24, G28, R20, R22, R24, R29, Y21, YG93
R22 ink refill
Colorless Blender (0)
19 inches ½-inch-wide white seam binding
Die templates: Standard Circles LG (#S4-114), Petite Scalloped Circles LG (#S4-115)
Die-cutting and embossing machine
Sandwich bag
Sewing machine with white thread
Adhesive foam tape
Paper adhesive

Materials

Cardstock: white smooth, black, white textured, blue
Paddington Kilburn printed paper
Stamps: Rock Idol, Rock My World
Black dye ink pad
Markers: B21, B24, B28, E21, E34, N-0, N-2, N-4, N-6, N-8, Y35, YR20, YR24
Black Multiliner
3 white brads
Die templates: Standard Circles LG (#S4-114), Standard Circles SM (#S4-116)
Die-cutting machine
Paper piercer
Adhesive foam tape
Paper adhesive

Rocker Boy

Design by **Colleen Schaan**

Techniques Used

- Flicking
- On-Paper Blending
- Transfer Blending

Coloring Instructions

1. Stamp boy onto white smooth cardstock.

2. Color skin with E21. Using Flicking technique, shade with E34; blend lightly.

3. Color hair with YR20. Using Flicking technique, shade with Y35 and YR24; do not blend.

4. Using On-Paper Blending technique, color jeans and alternating stripes on shirt with N-2, N-4 and N-6.

5. Using Flicking technique, shade white stripes and glass lenses with flicks of N-0 and N-2.

6. Using On-Paper Blending technique, color shoes with N-4, N-6 and N-8. **Note:** *Leave highlights white for more contrast.*

7. Using On-Paper Blending technique, color guitar and glasses with B21, B24 and B28.

8. Using a Transfer Blending technique, shade guitar strap and details with Y35 and YR24.

Assembly Instructions

Form a 4¼ x 5½-inch side-folded card from black cardstock.

Adhere a 3⅞ x 5⅛-inch piece of blue cardstock to white textured cardstock; trim a small border. Adhere to card front.

Stamp sentiment onto a 2 x 1⅛-inch piece of white smooth cardstock. Adhere to a 2 x 1¼-inch black piece of cardstock. Adhere to card front as shown.

Cut a 2 x 5⅛-inch piece from printed paper. Adhere to a 2⅛ x 5⅛-inch piece of white textured white cardstock. Pierce three holes through upper left corner of printed paper piece; insert brads. Adhere to card front as shown.

Using 2⅜-inch Standard Circles LG die template, die-cut a circle from white textured cardstock.

Using 2⅝-inch Standard Circles SM die template, die-cut a circle from black cardstock. Adhere white circle to black circle.

Cut out boy. Adhere to layered circles. Using Multiliner, draw a border along edge of white circle and sentimental panel. Attach to card front as shown with foam tape. ❧

Sources: *White smooth X-Press It Blending Card, markers and Multiliner from Imagination International Inc.; colored and textured cardstock from Bazzill Basics Paper Inc.; printed paper from 7gypsies; Rock Idol stamp from Sugar Nellie; Rock My World stamp from Hambo Stamps; Memento dye ink pad from Tsukineko LLC; die templates from Spellbinders™ Paper Arts; die-cutting machine from Sizzix.*

You Are Unique

Design by **Colleen Schaan**

Techniques Used

- One-Color Shading
- Flicking
- Transfer Blending
- Smooth Coloring

Coloring Instructions

1. Using black ink, stamp girls image onto a 2¾ x 2¾-inch piece of white smooth cardstock.

2. Using One-Color Shading technique, color and shade upper left girl with E53, upper right girl with E25, lower left girl with E00 and lower right girl with E000.

3. Color hair on upper left girl with N-0. Using Flicking technique, flick N-4 and N-6 on crown and tips; do not blend.

4. Using One-Color Shading technique, color and shade upper right girl with E59, lower left girl with YR12 and lower right girl with E08.

5. Using a Transfer Blending technique, color clothing with either BV00 and BV02, or R81 and R85.

6. Using Smooth Coloring technique, color background with B0000.

Assembly Instructions

Form a 4¼ x 5½-inch top-folded card from pink Dotted Swiss cardstock.

Cut a 4 x 5¼-inch piece from orange cardstock. Using gray ink, stamp sentiment onto lower right corner of orange panel. Adhere a 4 x 2¼-inch piece of printed paper to a 4 x 2½-inch piece of pink Dotted Swiss cardstock. Adhere to orange panel as shown.

Wrap a 6-inch length of ribbon around layered panel as shown; secure ends to back of orange piece.

Adhere girls image to pink Dotted Swiss cardstock and trim a narrow border. Adhere over layered panel as shown with foam tape.

Stack orange button on top of pink button. Slide white thread through stacked buttons; tie knot on front and trim ends. Pinch center on remaining length of ribbon; adhere to back of stacked buttons. Adhere to layered panel as shown. Adhere panel to card front. ✃

Sources: White smooth X-Press It Blending Card and markers from Imagination International Inc.; colored cardstock from Bazzill Basics Paper Inc.; stamp set from Stamping Bella; Memento dye ink pad from Tsukineko LLC.

Materials

Cardstock: white smooth, pink Dotted Swiss, orange
Pink printed paper
You Are Unique stamp set
Black dye ink pads: black, gray
Markers: B0000, BV00, BV02, E000, E00, E08, E25, E53, E59, N-0, N-4, N-6, R81, R85, YR12
9¾ inches 1½-inch-wide pink decorative wired ribbon
Buttons: large pink, orange
White thread
Adhesive foam tape
Paper adhesive

King of the Jungle

Design by Colleen Schaan

Techniques Used
- On-Paper Blending
- Transfer Blending
- Flicking

Coloring Instructions

1. Using black ink, stamp lion onto a 3¼ x 3¼-inch piece of white smooth cardstock.

2. Using On-Paper Blending technique, color body and face with E30, E33 and E35.

3. Color cheeks with E70. Using a Transfer Blending technique, shade with E71.

4. Color toes with E40. Using a Transfer Blending technique, shade with E42.

5. Using On-Paper Blending technique, color nose with R32, R35 and R39.

6. Color mane and tail tip with E53. Using Flicking technique, add shading with E55, E57 and E59; do not blend.

7. Using On-Paper Blending technique, color crown with Y11, Y15 and Y17.

8. Create ground by coloring a base with E43. Add dots of E44 and E49. Go over and soften by adding dots with Colorless Blender.

9. Using paintbrush and pigment paint, add highlights to toenails and nose.

Assembly Instructions

Form a 5½ x 4¼-inch top-folded card from dark brown cardstock.

Cut a 5¼ x 4-inch piece from yellow cardstock. Adhere a 5¼ x 1½-inch piece of printed cardstock to yellow panel as shown.

Wrap ribbon around yellow panel, over printed paper; tie knot on right side, trim ends. Adhere to card front.

Using brown ink, stamp sentiment onto white smooth cardstock. Cut a rectangle around sentiment. Adhere to dark brown cardstock; trim a small border.

Adhere lion panel to dark brown cardstock; trim a small border. Adhere sentiment panel to lion panel as shown. Using foam tape, attach to card front. ❧

Sources: *White smooth X-Press It Blending Card, markers, Colorless Blender and pigment paint from Imagination International Inc.; colored cardstock from Bazzill Basics Papers Inc.; Mirabelle Cardstock Pack from Hobby Lobby Stores Inc./The Paper Studio; King of the Jungle stamp from Whipper Snapper Designs Inc.; Wild Thing stamp set from Verve Stamps; Memento dye ink pads from Tsukineko LLC.*

Materials
Cardstock: white smooth, dark brown, yellow
Mirabelle Cardstock Pack
Stamps: King of the Jungle, Wild Thing set
Dye ink pads: black, brown
Markers: E30, E33, E35, E40, E42, E43, E44, E49, E53, E55, E57, E59, E70, E71, R32, R35, R39, Y11, Y15, Y17
Colorless Blender (0)
White pigment paint
14 inches ⅝-inch-wide hemp twine ribbon
Small paintbrush
Adhesive foam tape
Paper adhesive

Materials

Cardstock: white smooth, dark teal, green, yellow
12 x 12 In Brights paper pad
Stamps: Let the Day Begin, Kick Up Your Heels
Black dye ink pad
Markers: BG11, BG49, Y00, Y04, Y08, YG21, YG23, YG25, YG45, YR16
Black Multiliner
White pigment paint
2 white buttons
Deckled Mega Rectangles LG die templates (#S5-015)
Die-cutting machine
Small paintbrush
Paper adhesive

Kick Up Your Heels

Design by **Colleen Schaan**

Techniques Used

- On-Paper Blending
- Transfer Blending
- Smooth Coloring

Coloring Instructions

1. Stamp turtle onto a 3⅜ x 3¼-inch piece of white smooth cardstock.

2. Using On-Paper Blending technique, color face, legs and leaves with YG21, YG23 and YG25.

3. Color shell with BG11. Using a Transfer Blending technique, shade with BG49.

4. Using On-Paper Blending technique, color spots with Y00, Y04 and Y08.

5. Using Smooth Coloring technique, use small circles to color flower petals YR16 and flower center Y08.

6. Color ground with YG23. Add scribbles of YG45 and blend slightly.

7. Using paintbrush and pigment paint, add highlights to shell.

Assembly Instructions

Form a 5 x 5-inch top-folded card from green cardstock.

Adhere a 4⅝ x 4⅝-inch piece of plaid paper to dark teal cardstock; trim a small border. Adhere to card front.

Using 2⅞ x 6⅛-inch Deckled Mega Rectangles LG die template, die-cut a rectangle from dark teal cardstock. Trim down to a 4¾ x 2⅞-inch piece and adhere to card front as shown.

Adhere a 2 x 4⅝-inch piece of yellow cardstock to card front as shown.

Stamp "Kick up your heels!" onto upper right corner of turtle panel. Adhere to green cardstock; trim a small border. Adhere to card front as shown.

Using Multiliner, draw a dotted border around yellow panel and image panel as shown.

Adhere buttons to right edge of dark teal panel. ❧

Sources: *White smooth X-Press It Blending Card, markers, Multiliner and pigment paint from Imagination International Inc.; colored cardstock from Bazzill Basics Paper Inc.; paper pad from Martha Stewart Crafts; Let the Day Begin stamp from Whipper Snapper Designs Inc.; Kick Up Your Heels stamp from Hambo Stamps; Memento dye ink pad from Tsukineko LLC; die templates from Spellbinders™ Paper Arts; die-cutting machine from Sizzix.*

Materials

Cardstock: white smooth, teal, navy blue
  Dotted Swiss
Nottinghill Portobello printed paper
Stamps: Chester, Everyday Sayings set
Black dye ink pad
Markers: B97, BG72, E21, E25, E29, E33, N-0,
  N-2, N-4, N-6, N-8
Black Multiliner
2 white buttons
Blue hemp twine
Paper adhesive

Just a Note

Design by **Colleen Schaan**

Techniques Used

- Transfer Blending
- Flicking
- On-Paper Blending

Coloring Instructions

1. Stamp Chester onto a 2¾ x 4½-inch piece of white smooth cardstock.

2. Color skin with E21. Using a Transfer Blending technique, shade with E33.

3. Color hair with E25. Using Flicking technique, add shading with E29; do not blend.

4. Using On-Paper Blending technique, color pants, jacket, shoes and hat with N-0, N-2, N-4, N-6 and N-8 as desired.

5. Color vest with BG72. Add B97 to alternating diamonds with a tapping motion; do not blend.

Assembly Instructions

Form a 4¼ x 5½-inch top-folded card from teal cardstock. Layer and adhere a 4 x 5¼-inch piece of navy blue Dotted Swiss cardstock and a 4 x 2½-inch piece of Portobello paper to card front as shown.

Adhere Chester panel to teal cardstock; trim a small border. Stamp sentiment onto upper left corner of panel. Using Multiliner, draw a border along edges of panel. Adhere to card front.

Thread buttons with two lengths of twine; tie knots on front, trim ends. Adhere to card front as shown. ✎

Sources: White smooth X-Press It Blending Card, markers and Multiliner from Imagination International Inc.; colored cardstock from Bazzill Basics Paper Inc.; printed paper from 7gypsies; Chester stamp from Kraftin' Kimmie Stamps; Everyday Sayings stamp set from Hero Arts; Memento dye ink pad from Tsukineko LLC.

Siamese Strut

Design by **Colleen Schaan**

Technique Used
• Flicking

Coloring Instructions

1. Using black ink, stamp cats randomly onto a 3¾ x 3-inch piece of white smooth cardstock.

2. Color footpads and inner ears with E02.

3. Color cats with E40.

4. Using Flicking technique, add darker shades to feet, nose, ears and tail with E43 and E44; blend gently.

5. Shade ears and footpads with E40 and shade with E43.

Assembly Instructions

Form a 4¼ x 5½-inch top-folded card from blue/green Dotted Swiss cardstock.

Adhere cat panel to a 3⅞ x 5⅛-inch piece of light brown Dotted Swiss cardstock ¹⁄₁₆ inch below top edge. Adhere a 3¾ x 2-inch piece of printed paper to same light brown Dotted Swiss panel ¹⁄₁₆ inch above bottom edge. Adhere layered panel to kraft cardstock; trim a small border. Ink edges brown.

Using brown ink, stamp sentiment onto twill ribbon. Wrap twill around layered panel as shown; secure ends to back.

Cut a V-notch at one end of brown ribbon. Fold ribbon in half; adhere to layered panel as shown, securing un-notched end of ribbon to panel back. Allow V-notched edge of ribbon to extend past right edge of panel.

Pierce two holes through panel and insert brads as shown. Adhere to card front. ❧

Sources: *Cardstock from Bazzill Basics Paper Inc.; printed paper from Bo-Bunny Press; Farley Takes a Walk stamp from Eat Cake Graphics; Wild Thing stamp set from Verve Stamps; Memento dye ink pads from Tsukineko LLC; markers from Imagination International Inc.*

Materials

Cardstock: white smooth, kraft, blue/green
   Dotted Swiss, light brown Dotted Swiss
Learning Curve Recess printed paper
Stamps: Farley Takes a Walk, Wild Thing set
Dye ink pads: black, brown
Markers: E02, E40, E43, E44
Ribbon: 6 inches 1½-inch-wide cream twill,
   4½ inches ⅝-inch-wide brown grosgrain
2 light brown brads
Paper piercer
Paper adhesive

Materials

Cardstock: white smooth, black
Printed papers: Granola Honey, Basic Manila Glossary
Carpenter Joe digital stamp
Markers: B91, B95, B97, E11, E13, E25, E31, E35, E40, E42, E44, E47, N-0, N-2, N-4, Y23, Y28, YG91, YR12, YR14, YR18
Black Multiliner
2 Generation Z Metal Gears brads
Electronic cutting machine with All Occasions cartridge (#656160)
Die templates: Standard Circles SM (#S4-116), Standard Circles LG (#S4-114)
Die-cutting machine
Paper piercer
Paper adhesive
Computer with printer

My Hero

Design by **Colleen Schaan**

Techniques Used

- On-Paper Blending
- Flicking

Coloring Instructions

1. Print boy image onto white smooth cardstock.

2. Using On-Paper Blending technique, color skin with E11, E13 and E25.

3. Color hair with YR12. Using Flicking technique, add shading to hair with YR14, YR18 and Y28; do not blend.

4. Color board with E40. Shade with flicks of E42, E44 and E47; blend lightly.

5. Using On-Paper Blending technique, color jeans with B91, B95 and B97.

6. Using On-Paper Blending technique, color bib with Y23, E31, YG91 and E35.

7. Using On-Paper Blending technique, color toolbox with N-0, N-2 and N-4.

8. Color tools with YR12.

9. Color belt with E44

10. Add flicks of N-0 and N-2 to shirt and shoes for slight shadows.

11. Color ground with strokes of E40.

Assembly Instructions

Form a 5½ x 5½-inch top-folded card from black cardstock.

Cut a 5¼ x 5¼-inch piece from Honey paper; adhere a 5¼ x 2-inch piece of Glossary paper to Honey panel, ⅞ inch above bottom edge.

Trim boy panel down to a 3½ x 4¾-inch piece; adhere to black cardstock; trim a small border. Referring to photo, adhere to Honey panel at an angle.

Using 2⅛-inch Standard Circles SM die template, die-cut a circle from white smooth cardstock. Using 2⅜-inch Standard Circles LG die template, die-cut a circle from black cardstock. Layer and adhere circles to Honey panel.

Using electronic cutting machine and All Occasions cartridge, cut "My Hero" from black cardstock. Adhere to white circle.

Pierce holes and insert brads as shown. Adhere Honey panel to card front. Using black Multiliner, add a border around sentiment and image. ❧

Sources: *White smooth X-Press It Blending Card, markers and Multiliner from Imagination International Inc.; black cardstock from Bazzill Basics Paper Inc.; printed papers from BasicGrey; digital stamp from Tiddly Inks; brads from Little Yellow Bicycle; eclips electronic cutting machine with cartridge and die-cutting machine from Sizzix; die templates from Spellbinders™ Paper Arts.*

Materials
Cardstock: white smooth, natural cream,
  navy blue Dotted Swiss
Stamps: Pile of Teddies, Everyday Sayings
  set
Dye ink pads: black, light brown distress
Markers: B91, E11, E13, E15, E18, E21, E25,
  E30, E31, E33, E40, E42, E43, E50, E55,
  G94, N-4, N-6, N-8, R32, R37, YR16
Colorless Blender refill (0)
Black Multiliner
5 white brads
Stipple brush
Paper piercer
Adhesive foam tape
Paper adhesive

Warm Fuzzies

Design by **Colleen Schaan**

Techniques Used

- On-Paper Blending
- Transfer Blending

Coloring Instructions

1. Using black ink, stamp teddy bears onto a 5½ x 2½-inch piece of white smooth cardstock.

2. Working from left to right and using On-Paper Blending technique, color first bear with E11, E13 and E15.

3. Using a Transfer Blending technique, color first bear's feet E50 with E21.

4. Using On-Paper Blending technique, color second bear with E40, E42 and E43.

5. Color third bear with E21. Using a Transfer Blending technique, shade with E25.

6. Color third bear's stomach and feet with E50. Using a Transfer Blending technique, shade with E55.

7. Using On-Paper Blending technique, color fourth bear with E13, E15 and E18.

8. Using On-Paper Blending technique, color last bear with E30, E31 and E33.

9. Using On-Paper Blending technique, color bears' noses with N-4, N-6 and N-8.

10. Dip a stipple brush into Colorless Blender refill and tap off excess onto a paper towel. Tap brush onto colored bears to create texture.

11. Using a Transfer Blending technique, color flower petals with R32 and R37.

12. Color flower centers with YR16.

13. Color leaves with G94.

14. Add ground with strokes of B91.

Assembly Instructions

Form a 5½ x 4¼-inch top-folded card from natural cream cardstock. Ink edges light brown.

Cut a 5¼ x 4-inch piece from navy blue Dotted Swiss cardstock. Color brads with E25; let dry completely. Pierce five holes ⅜ inch above bottom edge of navy blue panel as shown. Insert colored brads in holes. Adhere to card front.

Ink edges of teddy bear panel light brown. Using Multiliner, draw a border along edge of panel as shown.

Using black ink, stamp "sending warm fuzzies" onto white smooth cardstock. Cut out sentiment; ink edges light brown. Adhere to top left back edge of teddy bear panel as shown. Adhere to card front. ❧

Sources: *White smooth X-Press It Blending Card, markers, Colorless Blender refill and Multiliner from Imagination International Inc.; colored cardstock from Bazzill Basics Paper Inc.; stamp from Whipper Snapper Designs Inc.; stamp set from Hero Arts; Memento dye ink pad from Tsukineko LLC; distress ink pad from Ranger Industries Inc.*

Materials

Cardstock: cream smooth, lime green, red
Pasta Fagioli printed papers: Meatballs, Clove Fresh Garlic
Stamp sets: Nerissa, Mermaid Sentiments
Black dye ink pad
Markers: B0000, E000, E00, E13, E17, E18, R02, R20, W-00, W-1, YG00, YG05, YR00
Colorless Blender (0)
2 lime green mini brads
¼-inch hole punch
Die templates: Standard Circles LG (#S4-114), Classic Scalloped Circles LG (#S4-124)
Die-cutting and embossing machine
Paper piercer
Adhesive foam tape
Paper adhesive

Something's Fishy

Design by **Michele Boyer**

Techniques Used

- On-Paper Blending
- Feathering

Coloring Instructions

1. Stamp mermaid onto cream smooth cardstock.

2. Color skin with E000; shade with E00. Color cheeks with R20 and eyelids with YG05.

3. Shade eyes with B0000; do not blend.

4. Using On-Paper Blending technique, color hair with E13, E17 and E18. Add more highlights by pulling out color from hair with Colorless Blender.

5. Using Feathering technique, color tail and shell with R02 and YR00. Add dots with YG05.

6. Using Feathering technique, color fins and top with YG00 and YG05.

7. Outline image with W-00 and W-1.

Assembly Instructions

Form a 5¼ x 5¼-inch top-folded card from lime green cardstock.

Adhere a 4⅞ x 4⅞-inch piece of Clove Fresh Garlic paper to red cardstock; trim a small border. Adhere a 3⅞ x 3⅞-inch piece of Meatballs paper to red cardstock; trim a small border. Layer and adhere printed paper panels to card front as shown.

Referring to photo, trim around top of mermaid's hair. Using 3¾-inch Standard Circles LG die template, die-cut and emboss a circle around mermaid, making sure to place die template under mermaid's cut-out hair. **Note:** *Trim into sides of mermaid as needed to slide die template under hair.* Adhere mermaid circle to red cardstock; trim a small border.

Using 4⅛-inch Scalloped Circles LG die template, die-cut a scalloped circle from lime green cardstock. Layer and adhere circles together. Attach to card front using foam tape.

Stamp "Something's" and "Fishy" onto cream cardstock. Cut out words. Adhere each word to red cardstock; trim small borders. Using ¼-inch hole punch, punch two circles from red cardstock. Pierce a hole through center of each punched circle; insert brads. Adhere a punched circle to left back edge of each sentiment. Attach to card front as shown. ❧

Sources: Cardstock from Bazzill Basics Paper Inc., WorldWin Papers and Papertrey Ink; printed papers from Jillibean Soup; stamp sets from Kraftin' Kimmie Stamps; Memento dye ink pad from Tsukineko LLC; markers and Colorless Blender from Imagination International Inc.; die templates from Spellbinders™ Paper Arts.

Raven Thanks

Design by **Colleen Schaan**

Technique Used
• On-Paper Blending

Coloring Instructions
Project note: Working with reds can be tricky. Use very little ink and let layers dry to avoid bleeding.

1. Stamp girl onto a 3 x 3¾-inch piece of white smooth cardstock.

2. Using On-Paper Blending technique, color jacket with R32, R35, R37, R39 and R59.

3. Create alternating stripes on scarf, hat and socks with R32. Shade with R39 and blend lightly with R35.

4. Using On-Paper Blending technique, color hat, boots, dress and alternating stripes with YR20, YR23 and YR24.

5. Use Colorless Blender to remove color from flowers on dress.

6. Add dots of R37 for flowers on dress.

7. Color hair and buttons with N-8.

8. Color skin with E50. Shade with E21 and lightly blend. Add dots of R02 for cheeks.

9. Add cast shadows to skin with BV00; add cast shadows to jacket with R59 and add cast shadows to dress with YR24.

Assembly Instructions
Form a 4¼ x 5½-inch top-folded card from red cardstock.

Adhere a 4 x 3½-inch piece of golden yellow cardstock to a 4 x 3⅝-inch piece of red cardstock. Adhere layered panel to a 4 x 5¼-inch piece of printed paper ⅜ inch above bottom edge. Machine-stitch around piece as shown. Adhere to card front.

Stamp sentiment onto lower right corner of image panel. Adhere to red cardstock; trim a small border. Machine-stitch along edges. Using foam tape, attach panel to card front. ꒰

Sources: *White smooth X-Press It Blending Card, markers and Colorless Blender from Imagination International Inc.; colored cardstock from Bazzill Basics Paper Inc.; printed paper from Cosmo Cricket; Raven stamp from Sugar Nellie; Everyday Sayings stamp set from Hero Arts; Memento dye ink pad from Tsukineko LLC.*

Materials
Cardstock: white smooth, red, golden yellow
Material Girl Calico printed paper
Stamps: Raven, Everyday Sayings set
Markers: BV00, E21, E50, N-8, R02, R32, R35, R37, R39, R59, YR20, YR23, YR24
Colorless Blender (0)
Sewing machine with golden yellow thread
Adhesive foam tape
Paper adhesive

Enchanting Friends

Design by **Beate Johns**

Materials
Cardstock: white smooth, rust, cream, black
Masking material
Noel Joy double-sided printed paper
Ophelia stamp set
Black dye ink pad
Markers: B0000, B000, B91, E00, E01, E08,
     E11, E13, E18, E19, E33, E35, E37, E39, E40,
     E41, E42, E44, E97, T-3, T-5, T-7, W-1, W-3,
     YG93, YG95, YG97, YG99, YR23, YR31
Colorless Blender (0)
Colorless Blender refill (0)
Clear glitter pen
Paper flower
Findings Adornments Charm pack:
     silver heart
2 silver small brads
Cream button
15 inches ½-inch-wide brown ribbon
7 inches ⅞-inch-wide cream decorative lace
Brown waxed linen thread
Paper piercer
Cloth or paper towel
Airbrush system
Sewing machine with white thread
Adhesive foam dots
Paper adhesive

Techniques Used
- On-Paper Blending
- Transfer Blending
- Feathering

Coloring Instructions
1. Stamp fairy and bird onto a 4⅛ x 4¾-inch piece of white smooth cardstock and onto masking material. Cut out fairy and bird from masking material and set aside to be used later.

2. Using On-Paper Blending technique, color rock with T-3, T-5 and T-7.

3. Apply Colorless Blender refill to a piece of cloth or paper towel and dab onto colored rock to create texture. Add dots back to rock with T-3, T-5 and T-7 to add texture.

4. Color skin with E00. Using a Transfer Blending technique, shade with E01, E11 and E13.

5. Color hair with E97. Using a Transfer Blending technique, shade with E08, E18 and E19; blend lightly.

6. Color bodice with E33. Using a Transfer Blending technique, shade with E35, E37 and E39.

7. Using On-Paper Blending technique, color skirt with YG93, YG95, YG97 and YG99.

8. Using On-Paper Blending technique, color body of bird with YR31, YR23 and E97.

9. Using a Transfer Blending technique, add YG93 and YG95 to bird's wings. Color over bird with a clear glitter pen.

10. Color fairy's wings with YR31. Go over wings with Colorless Blender to lighten. Using Feathering technique, add shading to wings by feathering YR31 and YR23 with W-1 and W-3. Add accents to wings with a clear glitter pen.

11. Add texture around image by dotting around image with B91, then B000 and B0000 for sky.

12. Add texture to ground by dotting ground with E40, E41, E42 and E44.

13. Mask image with cut-out images from step 1. Airbrush sky with B000 and ground with E41. Remove masking images.

Assembly Instructions
Form a 5½ x 6¼-inch top-folded card from rust cardstock.

Adhere a 5 x 5¾-inch piece of Joy paper, green side faceup, to cream cardstock; trim a small border. Adhere a 5 x 2-inch piece of Joy paper, brown side faceup, to layered panel ⅝ inch above bottom edge. With sewing machine, straight-stitch and zigzag-stitch around layered panel as desired.

Wrap lace around layered panel as shown, secure ends to back. Adhere to card front.

Adhere fairy panel to black cardstock; trim a small border. Machine-stitch around fairy panel. Attach to card front using foam dots.

Tie a double bow with ribbon. Thread heart charm with a long piece of waxed linen. Wrap waxed

linen thread around center of bow and thread through button and tie knot on front; trim ends. Adhere to card front as shown.

Stamp sentiment onto white smooth cardstock and cut out. Pierce a hole through each end of sentiment strip; insert brads. Adhere to card front as shown, using a foam dot on center to pop-up center of sentiment.

Adhere paper flower below right edge of sentiment. ❧

Sources: *White smooth X-Press It Blending Card, markers, Colorless Blender, Colorless Blender refill and airbrush system from Imagination International Inc.; colored cardstock from Stampin' Up!; printed paper from Bo-Bunny Press; stamp set from Kraftin' Kimmie Stamps; Memento dye ink pad from Tsukineko LLC; Recollections Boutique paper flower from Michaels Stores Inc.; silver heart charm from Ranger Industries Inc.*

Me Love You

Design by **Colleen Schaan**

Techniques Used
- On-Paper Blending
- Transfer Blending
- Flicking
- Feathering

Coloring Instructions

1. Print background image onto a 5 x 3¾-inch piece of white smooth cardstock.

2. Beginning with bushes in background and working your way forward, color each hedge with a different group of greens to make them stand out. Use following combinations and On-Paper Blending technique: YG91, YG93 and YG95; YG91, BG93 and BG96; YG91, YG63 and YG67. Create cast shadows with YG97.

3. Using On-Paper Blending technique, color tree trunks with E70, E71, E74 and E77.

4. Using a Transfer Blending technique, color plants with YG41 and YG45.

5. Using On-Paper Blending technique, color tree leaves with G00, G02, G05 and G07.

6. Color huts with Y11. Shade with YR20, Y23 and Y26. Using Flicking technique, flick each color from top down; do not blend.

7. Color insides of huts E79.

8. Using a Transfer Blending technique, color bamboo doors with E40 and E42.

9. Color door ties and trim E13.

10. Add dots of N-4 to bottoms of rocks. Add dots of N-2 and N-0 to blend.

11. Using Feathering technique, color fire Y11 and R27.

12. Color ground with E30. Add dots of E33 and E31. Add dots with Colorless Blender.

13. Stamp chief onto white smooth cardstock.

14. Color skin with E21. Using a Transfer Blending technique, add shading with E34.

15. Using On-Paper Blending technique, color mask with E34, E35 and E37.

16. Color grass skirt with Y11. Add flicks of YR20, Y23 and Y26; do not blend.

17. Using a Transfer Blending technique, color shirt with G02 and G05.

18. Using a Transfer Blending technique, color feathers with Y13 and Y17, YR12 and YR18, and R22 and R27.

Assembly Instructions

Form a 5½ x 4¼-inch top-folded card from black cardstock.

Adhere background image panel to white smooth cardstock; trim a small border. Adhere to card front. Stamp "ME LOVE YOU" in lower right corner of image panel.

Cut out chief image; attach to card front as shown using foam tape. ✄

Sources: *White smooth X-Press It Blending Card, markers and Colorless Blender from Imagination International Inc.; black cardstock from Bazzill Basics Paper Inc.; stamps from Hambo Stamps; Memento dye ink pad from Tsukineko LLC.*

Materials
Cardstock: white smooth, black
Stamps: Chief Hambooli, "Me Love You," Jungle background digital image
Black dye ink pad
Markers: BG93, BG96, E13, E21, E30, E31, E33, E34, E35, E37, E40, E42, E70, E71, E74, E77, E79, G00, G02, G05, G07, N-0, N-2, N-4, R22, R27, Y11, Y13, Y17, Y23, Y26, YG41, YG45, YG63, YG67, YG91, YG93, YG95, YG97, YR12, YR18, YR20
Colorless Blender (0)
Adhesive foam tape
Paper adhesive
Computer with printer

Materials

Cardstock: white smooth, brown, golden yellow
Nottinghill Westbourne printed paper
Stamps: Scratch My Back, Everyday Sayings set
Ink pads: black dye, light brown distress, dark brown distress
Markers: E08, E37, E50, E53, E55, E99, R32, R35, W-3, YG63, YG67, YR24
Colorless Blender (0)
Brown Multiliner
3 silver brads
Paper piercer
Paper adhesive

Necking

Design by **Colleen Schaan**

Techniques Used

- Transfer Blending
- On-Paper Blending
- Flicking

Coloring Instructions

1. Using black ink, stamp giraffes onto a 3½ x 4⅞ piece of white smooth cardstock.

2. Color each giraffe with E50.

3. Using a Transfer Blending technique, shade skin with E53.

4. Using On-Paper Blending technique, color each spot with YR24, E99 and E37.

5. Using tip, dab Colorless Bender onto spots to give a mottled effect.

6. Color hooves with E55. Using a Transfer Blending technique, shade with W-3.

7. Using a Transfer Blending technique, flick YG63 with YG67 onto leaves.

8. Using a Transfer Blending and Flicking technique, flick R32 with R35 onto flowers.

9. Add cast shadows with W-3.

Assembly Instructions

Form a 5½ x 5½-inch top-folded card from brown cardstock. Adhere a 5¼ x 5¼-inch piece of golden yellow cardstock to card front.

Cut a 4⅞ x 4⅞-inch piece from Westbourne paper. Adhere to brown cardstock; trim a small border. Adhere to card front.

Color brads with E08. Set aside to dry.

Adhere a 4⅞ x 2-inch piece of golden yellow cardstock to a 4⅞ x 2⅛-inch piece of brown cardstock. Pierce three holes along right side of layered piece. Insert dry colored brads into holes. Adhere to card front as shown.

Ink edges of giraffe panel light brown and dark brown. Using dark brown ink, stamp "XOXOXOX" onto upper right corner of panel. Using Multiliner, add a border along edges of panel. Adhere to a 3⅝ x 4⅞-inch piece of brown cardstock. Adhere to card front as shown. ❧

Sources: *White smooth X-Press It Blending Card, markers, Colorless Blender and Multiliner from Imagination International Inc; colored cardstock from Bazzill Basics Paper Inc.; printed paper from 7gypsies; Scratch My Back stamp from Whipper Snapper Designs Inc.; Everyday Sayings stamp set from Hero Arts; Memento dye ink pad from Tsukineko LLC; distress dye ink pads from Ranger Industries Inc.*

Love Letters

Design by Jennie Black

Technique Used
- On-Paper Blending

Coloring Instructions

1. Stamp image onto 4¾ x 3⅝-inch white smooth cardstock.

2. Using On-Paper Blending technique, color letters with E40, E41, E43, E44 and E49.

3. Using On-Paper Blending technique, color leaves with YG01, YG03 and YG63.

4. Using On-Paper Blending technique, color roses and bow with R22, R24 and R27.

Assembly Instructions

Form a 5½ x 4¼-inch top-folded card from brown cardstock.

Adhere image panel to red cardstock; trim a small border. Adhere to card front. ❧

Sources: White smooth X-Press It Blending Card and markers from Imagination International Inc.; colored cardstock from Bazzill Basics Paper Inc.; stamp from Peddler's Pack; Memento dye ink pad from Tsukineko LLC.

Materials

Cardstock: white smooth, brown, red
Love Letters Background stamp
Black dye ink pad
Markers: E40, E41, E43, E44, E49, R22, R24, R27, YG01, YG03, YG63
Paper adhesive

Heart Wreath

Design by **Colleen Schaan**

Techniques Used

- On-Paper Blending
- Flicking
- Transfer Blending

Coloring Instructions

1. Stamp heart wreath onto white smooth cardstock.

2. Using On-Paper Blending technique, color wreath with YR21, Y26 and Y28.

3. Using Flicking technique, add flicks of E99 to deepen shadows on wreath.

4. Using a Transfer Blending technique and Flicking technique, flick G40 with YG97 onto leaves.

5. Using On-Paper Blending technique, color ribbon with Y13, Y19 and YR15.

6. Using On-Paper Blending technique, color every third rose with R12, R14 and R17.

7. Using On-Paper Blending technique, color half of remaining roses with R22, R24 and R29; blend lightly.

8. Color remaining roses with R43. Using a Transfer Blending technique, shade with R46; blend lightly.

9. Using paintbrush, add highlights to flower centers and bow with pigment paint.

Assembly Instructions

Form a 5½ x 4¼-inch top-folded card from gold cardstock. Using Brackets die template, die-cut bottom edge of card front. Ink edges red/brown. Adhere a 5½ x 2-inch piece of printed paper inside card, aligning bottom edges.

Cut a 5½ x 1¾-inch piece from printed paper, die-cut bottom edge using Brackets die template. Adhere to card front as shown.

Adhere lace to card front as shown. Using black ink, stamp sentiment onto lower left corner of card front.

Using 3¾-inch Standard Circles LG die template, die-cut and emboss a circle around heart wreath. Leaving die template in place, use sponge to ink circle light brown. Remove die template. Attach to card front using foam tape. ❧

Sources: White smooth X-Press It Blending Card, markers and pigment paint from Imagination International Inc.; gold cardstock from Bazzill Basics Paper Inc.; Mirabelle paper pack from Hobby Lobby Stores Inc./The Paper Studio; Heart With Bow stamp set from Serendipity Stamps; Happy Spring stamp set from Gina K. Designs; Memento black dye ink pad from Tsukineko LLC; distress dye ink pads from Ranger Industries Inc.; Bracket die, and die-cutting and embossing machine from Sizzix; Standard Circles LG die templates from Spellbinders™ Paper Arts.

Materials

Cardstock: white smooth, gold
Mirabelle paper pack
Stamp sets: Heart With Bow, Happy Spring
Dye ink pads: black, red/brown distress, light brown distress
Markers: E99, G40, R12, R14, R17, R22, R24, R29, R43, R46, Y13, Y19, Y26, Y28, YG97, YR15, YR21
White pigment paint
5½ inches ¾-inch-wide ivory decorative lace
Die templates: Brackets (#656625), Standard Circles LG (#S4-114)
Die-cutting and embossing machine
Small paintbrush
Craft sponge
Adhesive foam tape
Paper adhesive

Friends are flowers in the *garden* of life

Materials

Cardstock: white smooth, dark sage green, light sage green, navy blue
Striped blue/brown printed paper
Stamps: Kroner, Quite a Catch set
Black dye ink pad
Markers: B32, B34, B37, E11, E13, E15, E21, E25, E41, E42, E43, E44, E57, N-2, N-4, R02, W-00, Y11, YG91, YG93, YR24
Colorless Blender (0)
Black Multiliner
Twine
Adhesive foam tape
Paper adhesive

Caught Ya!

Design by **Colleen Schaan**

Techniques Used

- On-Paper Blending
- Transfer Blending
- Flicking

Coloring Instructions

1. Stamp fisherman onto a 3½ x 4⅝-inch piece of white smooth cardstock.

2. Using On-Paper Blending technique, color skin with E11, E13 and E15.

3. Color fingernails with R02.

4. Using a Transfer Blending technique and Flicking technique, flick Y11 and YR24 onto hair and mustache.

5. Using On-Paper Blending technique, color hat with E42, E43 and E44.

6. Using a Transfer Blending technique, flick W-00 and E41 onto T-shirt from edges toward center.

7. Using On-Paper Blending technique, color jeans and hatband with B32, B34 and B37. Go over jeans very lightly with Colorless Blender to give them a stonewashed look.

8. Using On-Paper Blending technique, color belt and shoes with E21, E25 and E57.

9. Using On-Paper Blending technique, color jacket with E42, YG91, E43, E44 and YG93.

10. Using a Transfer Blending Technique, color fishing pole with N-2 and N-4 and E21 and E25.

11. For ground, add dots of varying size with E11, E42 and E44; do not blend.

Assembly Instructions

Form a 5½ x 5½-inch top-folded card from dark sage green cardstock. Adhere a 5½ x 3-inch piece of striped paper to a 5½ x 3¼-inch piece of light sage green cardstock. Wrap twine around layered panel three times; adhere to card front as shown.

Stamp sentiment onto upper right corner of fisherman panel; using Multiliner, draw a border along edges. Adhere panel to navy blue cardstock; trim a small border. Adhere to light sage green cardstock; trim a border. Using foam tape, attach to card front as shown. ❧

Sources: White smooth X-Press It Blending Card, markers, Colorless Blender and Multiliner from Imagination International Inc.; colored cardstock from Bazzill Basics Paper Inc.; Kroner stamp from Whipper Snapper Designs Inc.; Quite a Catch stamp set from Gina K. Designs; Memento dye ink pad from Tsukineko LLC.

Make It a Grande

Design by **Michele Boyer**

Techniques Used
- One-Color Shading
- Transfer Blending

Coloring Instructions

1. Stamp girl onto cream smooth cardstock.

2. Using One-Color Shading technique, color and shade hair with YR23.

3. Using One-Color Shading technique, color and shade dress, bow and shoes with YG93.

4. Color dress accents and socks with 100, YR23 and R27.

5. Color skin with E000. Using a Transfer Blending technique, shade with E00. Add R20 for cheeks.

6. Shade eyes with B0000. Do not blend.

7. Shade slip with E50.

8. Color cup and saucer with RV42. Using a Transfer Blending technique, shade with R27.

Assembly Instructions

Form a 5¼ x 5¼-inch top-folded card from sage green cardstock.

Adhere a 4¾ x 4¾-inch piece of Snow Pear paper to a 5 x 5-inch piece of sage green cardstock. Center and adhere a 4¾ x 3-inch piece of Oblate paper to layered panel. Stamp sentiment onto left side of layered panel as shown. Sprinkle with embossing powder; heat-emboss.

Adhere a 4¾ x ⅛-inch strip of sage green cardstock to layered panel along top edge of Oblate piece.

Cut a 4¾ x 1-inch piece of sage green cardstock. Die-cut scalloped edge along bottom edge. Adhere to layered panel along bottom edge of Oblate piece. Adhere lace to scalloped strip. Thread button with white twine; tie bow on front, trim ends. Adhere to bottom left of layered panel.

Cut out stamped image. Attach to layered panel using foam dots. Using foam dots, attach layered panel to card front. ❧

Sources: Cream smooth cardstock from Papertrey Ink; sage green cardstock from Bazzill Basics Paper Inc.; printed papers from BasicGrey; stamps from Kraftin' Kimmie Stamps; Memento dye ink pad from Tsukineko LLC; markers from Imagination International Inc.; Die-namics Small Scallop Border die from My Favorite Things.

Materials
Cardstock: cream smooth, sage green
Pyrus printed papers: Oblate, Snow Pear
Stamps: Gabrielle, Kimmie's Coffee
    Sentiments set
Black dye ink pad
Clear embossing powder
Markers: B0000, E000, E00, E50, R20, R27,
    RV42, YG93, YR23, 100
4¾ inches ⅝-inch-wide decorative
    cream lace
White twine
Large sage green button
Die-namics Small Scallop Border die
Die-cutting machine
Embossing heat tool
Adhesive foam dots
Paper adhesive

Let Your Light Shine

Design by Colleen Schaan

Materials
Cardstock: white smooth, red Dotted Swiss, blue
Mirabelle paper pack
Stamps: Light My Life digital, Swirly Stars set
Black dye ink pad
Markers: B32, B34, B37, C-3, C-5, C-7, E31, E35, E50, E55, E59, E95, E97, E99, G20, G21, G24, G28, R32, R35, R39, W-00, W-1, Y000
Black Multiliner
Curved Rectangles die templates (#S5-006)
Die-cutting machine
Adhesive foam tape
Paper adhesive
Computer with printer

Techniques Used
- On-Paper Blending
- Flicking
- Smooth Coloring

Coloring Instructions

1. Print lighthouse onto white smooth cardstock.

2. Using On-Paper Blending technique, color lighthouse roof and alternating stripes with R32, R35 and R39.

3. Using Flicking technique, shade alternating stripes with flicks of W-00 and W-1.

4. Using Smooth Coloring technique, color light Y000.

5. Using On-Paper Blending technique, color lighthouse with E95, E97 and E99.

6. Using On-Paper Blending technique, color roof with C-3, C-5 and C-7.

7. Color trees and grass with G20. Using squiggles, shade with G21, G24 and G28.

8. Color boat and dock with E31. Shade with flicks of E35.

9. Color land with E50. Add dots of E59 and then E55 to soften.

10. Add dots of B32, B34 and B37 to water; do not blend.

Assembly Instructions

Form a 4¼ x 5½-inch top-folded card from red Dotted Swiss cardstock. Adhere a 4¼ x 3½-inch piece of blue cardstock to card front as shown.

Using 3 x 4½-inch Curved Rectangles die template, die-cut rectangle around image. Using Multiliner, draw a wavy border along edges. Attach to card front using foam tape.

Stamp sentiment onto white smooth cardstock. Using Multiliner, create a dotted border around sentiment as shown. Cut out sentiment; adhere to red Dotted Swiss cardstock; trim a small border. Adhere to die-cut image as shown. ✍

Sources: *White smooth X-Press It Blending Card, markers and Multiliner from Imagination International Inc.; Dotted Swiss and blue cardstock from Bazzill Basics Paper Inc.; Mirabelle paper pack from Hobby Lobby Stores Inc./ The Paper Studio; digital stamp from Tiddly Inks; stamp set from Verve Stamps; Memento dye ink pad from Tsukineko LLC; die templates from Spellbinders™ Paper Arts; die-cutting machine from Sizzix.*

Contributors

About the Authors

Colleen Schaan is a Regional Copic Certification Instructor and team member of the Fine Art Education program in North America and travels extensively across the nation for workshops, demos and trade shows. She holds English and secondary education degrees from Wartburg College and taught English at the middle school, high school and college levels for 12 years before retiring to focus on a career in creative arts. She currently resides in Atlanta, Ga., with her husband and three fur babies.

Marianne Walker is the Product Director for Imagination International Inc., where she develops product publications and certification manuals. She is the Lead Illustrator for Our Craft Lounge and the author of *Shadows & Shading, A Beginner's Guide to Lighting*. She travels throughout the United States teaching drawing and coloring classes at trade shows, stores and art schools. She graduated from the University of Oregon with a bachelor of fine arts in multimedia design and a minor in journalism/advertising. She currently resides in Springfield, Ore., with her husband and two children.

Copic is a registered trademark of Too Corporation, Japan

Buyer's Guide

7gypsies
(877) 412-7467
www.sevengypsies.com

BasicGrey
(801) 544-1116
www.basicgrey.com

Bazzill Basics Paper Inc.
(800) 560-1610
www.bazzillbasics.com

Bo-Bunny Press
(801) 771-4010
www.bobunny.com

C.C. Designs Rubber Stamps
(423) 949-6668
www.allthatscraps.com

Cosmo Cricket
(800) 852-8810
www.cosmocricket.com

Crate Paper Inc.
(801) 798-8996
www.cratepaper.com

Eat Cake Graphics
(831) 638-1223
www.eatcakegraphics.com

Echo Park Paper Co.
(800) 701-1115
www.echoparkpaper.com

Elisabeth Bell Designs
www.elisabethbell.com

Fiskars
(866) 348-5661
www.fiskarscrafts.com

Flourishes
(850) 475-1500
www.flourishes.org

Gina K. Designs
(608) 579-1026
www.ginakdesigns.com

Glitz Design
(866) 356-6131
www.glitzitnow.com

Hambo Stamps
www.hambostamps.com

Hero Arts
(800) 822-HERO (822-4376)
www.heroarts.com

**Hobby Lobby Stores Inc./
The Paper Studio**
www.hobbylobby.com

Imagination International Inc.
(541) 684-0013
www.copicmarker.com

**Janlynn Corp./
Stamps Happen Inc.**
www.janlynn.com

Jenni Bowlin Studio
www.jbsmercantile.com

Jillibean Soup
(888) 212-1177
www.jillibean-soup.com

JustRite
www.justritestampers.com

Kaisercraft
(888) 684-7147
www.kaisercraft.net

KI Memories
(972) 243-5595
www.kimemories.com

Kraftin' Kimmie Stamps
www.kraftinkimmiestamps.com

Layers of Color
(425) 835-2408
www.layersofcolor.com

Little Yellow Bicycle
(860) 286-0244
www.mylyb.com

Lockhart Stamp Co.
(707) 775-4703
www.lockhartstampcompany.com

Martha Stewart Crafts
www.marthastewartcrafts.com

Memory Box
www.memoryboxco.com

Michaels Stores Inc.
(800) MICHAELS (642-4235)
www.michaels.com

My Favorite Things
www.mftstamps.com

October Afternoon
(866) 513-5553
www.octoberafternoon.com

Our Craft Lounge
(877) 44-LOUNGE (445-6864)
www.ourcraftlounge.net

Papertrey Ink
www.papertreyink.com

Peddler's Pack
(503) 641-9555
www.peddlerspack.com

Pink Paislee
(816) 729-6124
www.pinkpaislee.com

Provo Craft
(800) 937-7686
www.provocraft.com

Ranger Industries Inc.
(732) 389-3535
www.rangerink.com

Serendipity Stamps
(816) 532-0740
www.serendipitystamps.com

Sizzix
(877) 355-4766
www.sizzix.com

Spellbinders™ Paper Arts
(888) 547-0400
www.spellbinderspaperarts.com

Stampin' Up!
(800) STAMP UP (782-6787)
www.stampinup.com

Stamping Bella
(866) 645-2355
www.stampingbella.com

Sugar Nellie
www.sugarnellie.com

Tiddly Inks
www.tiddlyinks.com

Tsukineko LLC
(800) 769-6633
www.tsukineko.com

Verve Stamps
www.shopverve.com

Whipper Snapper Designs Inc.
(262) 938-6824
www.whippersnapperdesigns.com

WorldWin Papers
www.worldwinpapers.com

Zva Creative
(801) 243-9281
www.zvacreative.com

*The Buyer's Guide listings are provided
as a service to our readers and should
not be considered an endorsement from
Annie's Attic.*